Collins

AQA GCSE
English Language
and English Literature

Advanced Student Book

Series Editors: Sarah Darragh and Jo Heathcote

Sarah Darragh
Phil Darragh
Mike Gould
Jo Heathcote

William Collins' dream of knowledge for all began with the publication of his first book in 1819. A self-educated mill worker, he not only enriched millions of lives, but also founded a flourishing publishing house. Today, staying true to this spirit, Collins books are packed with inspiration, innovation and practical expertise. They place you at the centre of a world of possibility and give you exactly what you need to explore it.

Collins. Freedom to teach

HarperCollins Publishers
1 London Bridge Street
London SE1 9GF
HarperCollins *Publishers*
1st Floor
Watermarque Building
Ringsend Road
Dublin 4
Ireland

Browse the complete Collins catalogue at www.collins.co.uk

First edition 2015

10 9 8 7 6

© HarperCollins Publishers 2015

ISBN 978-0-00-759680-5

Collins® is a registered trademark of HarperCollins Publishers Limited

www.collins.co.uk

A catalogue record for this book is available from the British Library

Commissioned by Catherine Martin and Emily Pither
Project managed by Hamish Baxter
Project management and editing by Lesley Gray
Edited by Catherine Dakin
Proofread by Claire Throp
Designed and typeset by Ken Vail Graphic Design
Cover design by We are Laura
Printed and bound by CPI Group (UK) Ltd, Croydon, CR0 4YY

Approval message from AQA

This textbook has been approved by AQA for use with our qualification. This means that we have checked that it broadly covers the specification and we are satisfied with the overall quality. Full details of our approval process can be found on our website.

We approve textbooks because we know how important it is for teachers and students to have the right resources to support their teaching and learning. However, the publisher is ultimately responsible for the editorial control and quality of this book.

Please note that when teaching the GCSE English Language and English Literature course, you must refer to AQA's specification as your definitive source of information. While this book has been written to match the specification, it does not provide complete coverage of every aspect of the course.

A wide range of other useful resources can be found on the relevant subject pages of our website: www.aqa.org.uk.

Contents

Chapter 7 • Comparing texts

English Language AO3 • English Literature AO2

7.1 Compare how writers use tone to convey viewpoints and perspectives

7.2 Compare the influence of poetic voices over time

7.3 Compare and evaluate how writers explore similar ideas in poetry

7.4 Apply your skills to English Language and English Literature tasks

Chapter 8 • Writing creatively

English Language AO5, AO6

8.1 Engage the reader through original forms of narration

8.2 Use imagery and symbolism to enhance narrative and descriptive power

8.3 Use structures to create memorable texts

8.4 Apply your skills to an English Language task

Chapter 9 • Point of view writing

English Language AO5, AO6

9.1 Convey convincing and original voices in your writing

9.2 Manipulate structure to create effects in point-of-view writing

9.3 Match style and tone to purpose and audience

9.4 Apply your skills to an English Language task

Introduction

The Collins AQA GCSE English Language and GCSE English Literature Advanced Student Book is designed to develop the skills required for GCSE English Language and GCSE English Literature.

The book is structured on the principle that very similar skills underpin success in both English Language and English Literature. The chapters address the GCSE Assessment Objectives in turn, revisiting the skills covered in the Core Student Book at a more sophisticated level and showing you how to make progress as you apply them to a range of reading and writing tasks.

You will notice that each chapter focuses on a maximum of two Assessment Objectives – usually one from GCSE English Language, and one from GCSE English Literature. This is because, although the two qualifications are separate, the skills are usually exactly the same. Within individual lessons, where relevant to the ideas being explored, additional AOs are referenced to emphasise the inter-relationships between the different skills being taught.

You will be encouraged to read a wide range of challenging literary and non-literary fiction and non-fiction texts, as you strengthen the ways in which you read for meaning, and analyse and evaluate writers' choices. You will also develop your ability to write convincingly for a range of different purposes, communicating your ideas not only accurately and effectively but with originality and flair.

This approach should give you the confidence to tackle unseen texts in your GCSE English Language and GCSE English Literature exams, and will support you as you explore and write in depth about the novels, plays and poems you are studying for GCSE.

How the book is structured

The first two chapters of the book introduce you to some fundamental skills and concepts which you will build upon as you progress through your GCSE course.

Chapter 1 is called 'Key technical skills' because these skills are indeed 'key' to being able to communicate effectively, and also to developing a deeper understanding of the ways in which other writers convey their own ideas. Accuracy is a very important part of the new GCSEs and we have put this chapter first to remind you that whenever you are using the written word, it is really important to do so with precision and technical accuracy.

Chapter 2 then introduces some of the 'Key concepts' you need to understand for GCSE study. This chapter also introduces you to different styles of writing and reminds you of some important principles to think about as you progress further through the book.

Chapters 3–7 focus more closely on how to read and how to write in a sophisticated and convincing way about what you have read. As simple as this may sound, the chapters are designed to ensure that you become a discerning, critical reader of a range of written genres and styles. The chapters build from simpler skills such as comprehension and inference to more advanced skills such as analysing and evaluating the effect of writers' choices. Finally, you will learn how to apply these skills in combination to more complex tasks when producing an extended critical response or a comparison of two texts.

Chapters 8 and 9 focus on helping you become an effective writer, whether you are writing creatively or presenting a point of view. You will look at how to communicate nuances and shades of meaning through your choice of words, your thoughtful or original choice of structure and form, and how to manipulate what you write to achieve a specific purpose or effect.

How to use the book

Each chapter is divided into a sequence of 'topics' or lessons. The lessons introduce, build and extend the skills identified at the start of the chapter.

a big question to think about at the start of the lesson and to try to answer at the end of the lesson

clear learning objectives

at-a-glance match to the specification

defines key terminology

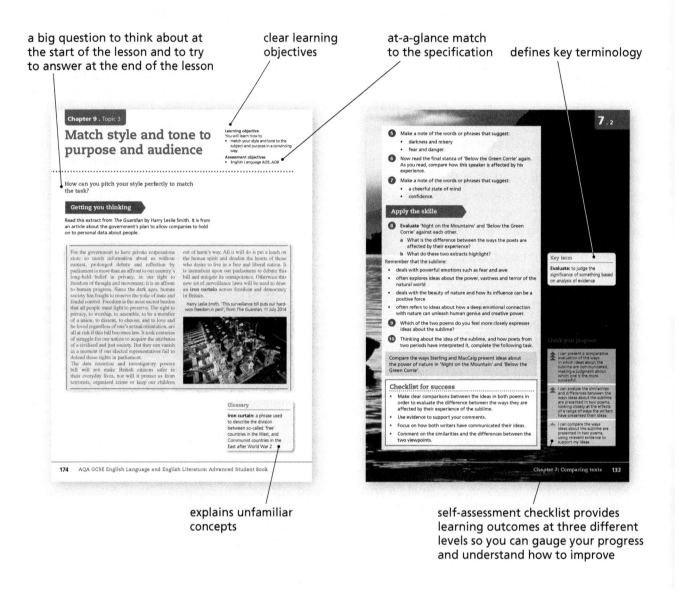

explains unfamiliar concepts

self-assessment checklist provides learning outcomes at three different levels so you can gauge your progress and understand how to improve

The skills-building sequences lead up to a substantial, synoptic 'Apply your skills' task or series of tasks at the end of each chapter. You can use this to assess your progress, as sample responses at two levels are provided for you to judge your own work against.

We hope that you enjoy using this book, and that it helps you to make the progress that you need to successfully complete your GCSE English Language and GCSE English Literature course.

Sarah Darragh and Jo Heathcote
Series editors

Chapter 1
Key technical skills

What's it all about?

In this chapter, you will learn some of the key technical skills in English. You will learn more about phrases and their grammatical uses. You will also look at how sentences are formed and structured to create effects and learn some of the correct technical terms to help you in your studies. This knowledge will underpin your work in later chapters, particularly Chapters 4, 6, 8 and 9.

In this chapter, you will learn

- an introduction to phrases
- sentence structures and punctuation
- structural effects in sentences.

	English Language GCSE	English Literature GCSE
Which AOs are covered?	AO2 Communicate clearly, effectively and imaginatively, selecting and adapting tone, style and register for different forms, purposes and audiences. Organise information and ideas, using structural and grammatical features to support coherence and cohesion of texts AO6 Use a range of vocabulary and sentence structures for clarity, purpose and effect, with accurate spelling and punctuation	AO2 Analyse the language, form and structure used by a writer to create meanings and effects, using relevant subject terminology where appropriate AO4 Use a range of vocabulary and sentence structures for clarity, purpose and effect, with accurate spelling and punctuation
How will this be tested?	Some questions will ask you to focus in detail on particular words and phrases. Others will identify a particular area of a text and ask you to look closely at the meanings and techniques being used in that particular part. All the texts you will be responding to will be previously unseen. You will be asked to complete writing tasks under timed conditions and will need to be able to use and punctuate varied sentences to create effects.	Wider questions will ask you to analyse and comment on the overall text, paying attention to the structure or the literary techniques being used by the writer to communicate meanings and create effects. Sometimes you will be responding to a whole play or novel that you have studied in class and sometimes you will be writing about two previously unseen poems.

An introduction to phrases

Learning objective
You will learn to
- explore different types of phrases and how they create meaning in texts.

Assessment objectives
- English Language AO2, AO6
- English Literature AO2, AO4

Isn't a **phrase** just a cluster of words?

Getting you thinking

Just like words have different roles to play within a sentence, so do phrases. The type of phrase that a writer chooses can help to create more specific meanings and effects for readers.

Noun phrases

One of the most well-used phrase types is the noun phrase.

A noun phrase is a combination of adjective(s) + a noun usually preceded by 'a', 'the' or 'some'.

> **Key term**
>
> **phrase:** two or more words forming a complete expression or forming part of a sentence

1 Look at the following examples and jot down some notes as to what you see in your mind's eye in each case.

a the sunlit garden	**a** some dappled waves	**a** a black starry night
b the moonlit garden	**b** some crashing waves	**b** a black stormy night

Whenever you change the adjective in the noun phrase, you change the mental picture you have in your head. This is known as **modification.**

2 Look back at the noun phrases in Activity 1. If those noun phrases were used in a story, how might the mood be different between phrase **a** and **b** in each case?

> **Key term**
>
> **modification:** when the mental picture we have of the noun is altered by the choice of the adjective or other forms which accompany it

Explore the skills

Adjectival phrases

Sometimes, it *can* be more effective to use a group of words to do the job of an adjective.

For example:

> *The sunlit garden...* could be more beautiful as... *the garden was bathed in sunlight.*
>
> *The starry night...* could be more atmospheric as... *the night sky was filled with stars.*

A group of words, used in this way to replace a single adjective, is known as an **adjectival phrase**.

> **Key term**
>
> **adjectival phrase:** a group of words that describe a noun

3 Experiment with the effect adjectival phrases can create by writing the opening paragraph to a short story. Below are nine sentences which all contain adjectives:

He was a tall man.	He was in a side street.
He stood under the orange streetlamp.	There were deserted warehouses.
He wore a grey wool suit.	There was a brand new Mercedes.
He had a steely gaze.	It had dipped headlights.
It was a cloudless night.	

Rewrite the sentences, replacing the adjectives with adjectival phrases. Use them to continue the following short story. The first two have been done for you as an example.

> Jack Strangelove was a man of great height. He stood under the streetlamp's glow of orange, looking every inch the business man…

4 Look over your finished story opening. What additional effects do you think you have created by using adjectival phrases?

Prepositions and prepositional phrases

Locating things in time and place is done through the use of **prepositions**.

5 Some of our most common prepositions are included in the box below. Note down six more of your own.

about	above	among	around	below	beneath
between	by	down	from	in	near	of	over
through	under	until	upon	with	

Key term

prepositions: words which are used to show the relation of one noun or pronoun to another in a sentence

6 The poet John Donne used prepositions to create effect in his poem 'To His Mistris going to Bed' in 1654, where he used an image of exploring new lands to describe his lover.

a Identify the prepositions in the extract.

b How does Donne link the prepositions to the image of exploration?

> **To His Mistris going to Bed**
>
> Licence my roving hands, and let them go,
> Before, behind, between, above, below.
> O my America! my new-found-land,
> My kingdom, safeliest when with one man mann'd,
> My Mine of precious stones, My Empirie,
> How blest am I in this discovering thee!
>
> John Donne

When prepositional phrases are used, they often help you answer the key questions of *where, when, how, what, which* and *whose*. By identifying the prepositional phrases, you can often work out key ideas – especially when dealing with an unseen text.

7 Look at the following extract from the poem 'Daffodils' by William Wordsworth. Answer the questions in the annotations by focusing on the information in the prepositional phrases, which have been highlighted for you.

Daffodils

I wandered lonely as a cloud
That floats on high o'er vales and hills, **1**
When all at once **2** I saw a crowd,
A host, of golden daffodils;
Beside the lake, beneath the trees, **3**
Fluttering and dancing in the breeze. **4**

Continuous as the stars **5** that shine
And twinkle on the Milky Way, **6**
They stretched in never-ending line **7**
Along the margin of a bay:
Ten thousand saw I at a glance, **8**
Tossing their heads in sprightly dance. **9**

William Wordsworth

1 What type of cloud does Wordsworth want you to picture?

2 How does this prepositional phrase connected to time show the impact the daffodils make on Wordsworth?

3 How do these prepositional phrases help you to imagine the quantity of daffodils in the landscape?

4 How is a sense of movement created and what sort of movement do you imagine?

5 How does this help us picture the number of flowers?

6 How does this add to the beauty of the image?

7 What sense is created here?

8 What speed is conveyed here? How does this help us see Wordsworth's message about natural beauty?

9 How does he capture the innocence and beauty of the flowers here?

> **Develop the skills**

Adverbials and adverbial phrases

A further way of helping us to get a sense of time, place or manner in a text is through the use of adverbials.

Like adjectival phrases, an adverbial phrase is when two or more words do the job of an **adverb**. For example:

- The baby slept *soundly.* (adverb of manner)
- The baby slept *in peace.* (adverbial phrase of manner)

8 Rewrite the following sentences, changing the adverbs to adverbial phrases to make them more interesting.

   a I'll do my homework quickly.
   b The stars shone brightly.
   c In our town it rains constantly.
   d The boy acted foolishly.
   e I go to the gym regularly.

Now look at this further example:

The baby cried *like a lamb bleating.*

When the adverbial contains another noun (a lamb) and verb (bleats), it becomes an **adverbial clause.**

9 Read the poem by William Blake, which is made up entirely of adverbial clauses, except for the final two lines. Think about the effect this creates before answering the questions below.

   a What image of the natural world does Blake create through the adverbial clauses?

   b What kind of a 'time' is created through the adverbial clauses? How would you describe it?

   c When Blake invites his love to 'Come live, and be merry, and join with me', how is this made more innocent than in the Donne poem in Activity 6, because of the adverbial clauses in the rest of the poem?

Key term

adverb: a word that changes or simplifies the meaning of a verb, and usually answers how or when an action was done (for example, *angrily*, *later*)

Key term

adverbial clause: a subordinate clause that does the job of an adverb. The entire clause can modify a verb, an adjective or even another adverb

Laughing Song

When the green woods laugh with the voice of joy,
And the dimpling stream runs laughing by;
When the air does laugh with our merry wit,
And the green hill laughs with the noise of it;

When the meadows laugh with lively green,
And the grasshopper laughs in the merry scene,
When Mary and Susan and Emily
With their sweet round mouths sing 'Ha, ha, he!'

When the painted birds laugh in the shade,
Where our table with cherries and nuts is spread,
Come live, and be merry, and join with me,
To sing the sweet chorus of 'Ha, ha, he!'

William Blake

Check your progress:

▲▲ I can recognise different types of phrases, use them to work out the precise inferences and effects that a writer creates, as well as apply them in my own work for effect

▲ I can recognise different types of phrases, comment on their use in reading and include a variety of them in my writing.

▲ I can recognise the names of different types of phrases and can use some of them in my writing.

Apply the skills

10 Now use your knowledge on the different types of phrases to attempt the following task.

Think of a person or place you know well. Create a snapshot poem of that person or place using lines which contain the following phrase types:

Line 1: Noun phrase
Line 2: Adjectival phrase
Line 3: Prepositional phrase
Line 4: Adverbial phrase or clause
Line 5: Noun phrase.

Sentence structures and punctuation

Learning objective
You will learn to
• explore the structure of sentences and more complex punctuation.
Assessment objectives
• English Language AO2, AO6
• English Literature AO2, AO4

Some texts use very complex sentences – how do you 'unpack' them?

Getting you thinking

Many students think that the term **complex sentence** refers to how difficult a sentence is to understand – but you have probably been reading complex sentences since you first began reading.

Look at the following extract from the opening of a children's novel by J.K. Rowling.

> When Mr and Mrs Dursley woke up on the dull, grey Tuesday morning our story starts, there was nothing about the cloudy sky outside to suggest that strange and mysterious things would soon be happening all over the country. **1** Mr Dursley hummed as he picked out his most boring tie for work and Mrs Dursley gossiped away happily as she wrestled a screaming Dudley into his high chair. **2**
>
> None of them noticed a large tawny owl flutter past the window. **3**
>
> At half past eight, Mr Dursley picked up his briefcase, pecked Mrs Dursley on the cheek and tried to kiss Dudley goodbye but missed, because Dudley was now having a tantrum and throwing his cereal at the walls. **4**
>
> J.K. Rowling, from *Harry Potter and the Philosopher's Stone*

The four main ways we can structure sentences in English are named:

• **simple sentence**
• **compound sentence**
• **complex sentence**
• **compound-complex sentence**.

1. Look back at the sentences in the extract.
   a. Note down the different ideas in sentences 1 and 4. What is the main idea in each? What additional details are given?
   b. How many things are happening in sentence 2 and how are they connected? Who is doing the things? What is the subject of each verb in the sentence?
   c. In which sentence is there only one main idea? What effect does that have?
   d. Decide which label might belong with which sentence and why.

Key term

complex sentence: develops ideas in a simple sentence and adds detail and information in subsections known as subordinate clauses

Key terms

simple sentence: presents one idea. It will have one verb or verb phrase and contain one action, event or state

compound sentence: two simple sentences with linked ideas joined together with conjunctions (*and, or, but*)

compound-complex sentence: a complex sentence connected to a simple sentence by a conjunction

Explore the skills

Simple sentences are not necessarily 'easy to read' or understand. The simplicity is linked to their structure, not their ideas.

2   Look at the following extract from *The Waves,* a novel by Virginia Woolf. What situation is being described in this extract that is constructed in simple sentences? Make a note of your ideas.

> I am left alone to find an answer. The figures mean nothing now. Meaning has gone. The clock ticks. The two hands are convoys marching through a desert. The black bars on the clock are green oases. The long hand has marched ahead to find water. The other painfully stumbles among hot stones in the desert. It will die in the desert.
>
> Virginia Woolf, from *The Waves*

3   Now look at this extract from the same novel.

> Now taking her lump of chalk she draws figures, six, seven, eight, and then a cross and then a line on the blackboard. What is the answer? The others look; they look with understanding. Louis writes; Susan writes; Neville writes; Jinny writes; even Bernard has now begun to write. But I cannot write.

It contains some far more difficult sentence structures, but it comes *before* the extract in Activity 2.

a   How does this extract help you to understand the previous one?

b   What does it explain for you?

Develop the skills

A complex sentence still has, at its core, a simple sentence. However, it develops the idea contained in the simple sentence known as the *main clause*. It adds more detail and information in little subsections known as the *subordinate clauses* as they can't make sense alone, without the main one.

When we read older texts, particularly those from the nineteenth century, we often have to unpack highly complex sentence structures.

Punctuation is also used in a complex way but it is designed to create pauses as we read. It separates the different elements in the 'thought journey' for us. It is important to read and use the clues in the punctuation to identify the main clause – the main idea – in each sentence.

4 The main punctuation marks we find in complex sentences are listed in the following chart. Examples are given of them in both creative writing and analytical writing.

   a Work out what the punctuation marks are doing in each case before writing your own definition of their role.

   b Then, practise using the punctuation marks by completing the chart.

	Definition	In creative writing	In analysis
Comma	To separate the main clause from the subordinate clauses		As well as being a dramatist, Shakespeare wrote sonnets, many of which were about love.
Semicolon	To join together two main clauses which have a link, instead of a conjunction	The train grudgingly pulled out of the station; we were going to war.	
Pairs of commas, pairs of dashes (parenthesis)	Used to add an explanation or an afterthought into a sentence		Blake wrote many poems about religion – though he was against organised religion himself – and the theme of spirituality can be seen in…
Colon	Used to introduce an explanation, description or list related to what has come before	Peterson checked out the room, mentally recording all he could see: burnt CDs, recording equipment, laptop and fresh milk on the counter. Someone had been here recently.	

When reading long complex sentences, it's useful to follow these 'stage directions' for the punctuation marks.

Comma	Take a micro pause
Semicolon	Leave a longer pause – it may be separating parts that *could* have been separate sentences or joined by a conjunction
Pairs of commas, pairs of dashes (parenthesis)	Pause for both – it's introducing an aside
Colon	Stop for two seconds! It's a signal to look ahead – it is about to introduce something like a dialogue or list of related items
Full stop	You can stop for a few seconds. Phew!

5 In the following extract from *Pride and Prejudice* by Jane Austen, Elizabeth has just discovered her sister Lydia has eloped. Elizabeth has fallen in love with Mr Darcy, who is with her when she discovers the news, but feels this family disgrace will threaten her own future.

Read this extract aloud. Use the punctuation 'stage directions' to help you.

> Lydia – the humiliation, the misery, she was bringing on them all – soon swallowed up every private care; and covering her face with her handkerchief, Elizabeth was soon lost to every thing else; and, after a pause of several minutes, was only recalled to a sense of her situation by the voice of her companion, who, in a manner, which though it spoke compassion, spoke likewise restraint, said, 'I am afraid you have been long desiring my absence, nor have I any thing to plead in excuse of my stay, but real, though unavailing, concern. Would to heaven that any thing could be either said or done on my part, that might offer consolation to such distress! But I will not torment you with vain wishes, which may seem purposely to ask for your thanks. This unfortunate affair will, I fear, prevent my sister's having the pleasure of seeing you at Pemberley to-day.'
>
> Jane Austen, from *Pride and Prejudice*

6 **a** Copy and complete the map of the thought journey through the extract, which is all one sentence.

 b Then look back at the passage to Darcy's dialogue. How many separate ideas can you identify and 'map'?

<u>Main clause</u>
The news about Lydia has made Elizabeth forget her own problems.

Quotation = 'Lydia – the humiliation, the misery, she was bringing on them all – soon swallowed up every private care;'

Separated by: a semicolon

Additional ideas:
1. Lydia has brought a lot of shame to the family.
 Quotation = ...
 Separated by: pair of dashes

2. ....
 Quotation = 'and covering her face with her handkerchief, Elizabeth was soon lost to everything else;'
 Separated by: ....

3. After a few minutes Darcy's voice brings her back to reality
 Quotation = ...
 Separated by: ....

4. ....
 Quotation = 'who, in a manner, which though it spoke compassion, spoke likewise restraint, said,'
 Separated by: ....

Apply the skills

7 Using your experience of mapping thought journeys, attempt the following task.

Map the thought journey in this next sentence from *Pride and Prejudice*, starting with the main idea. Use a dictionary to look up any vocabulary you are unsure of.

> As he quitted the room, Elizabeth felt how improbable it was that they should ever see each other again on such terms of cordiality as had marked their several meetings in Derbyshire; and as she threw a retrospective glance over the whole of their acquaintance, so full of contradictions and varieties, sighed at the perverseness of those feelings which would now have promoted its continuance, and would formerly have rejoiced in its termination.

Check your progress:

⬆ I can understand how to decode the most complex sentences to extract key meanings and how to use different sentence types to create precise meanings in my own work.

⬆ I can understand how each sentence type is constructed and how to use them in my own work for effect.

⬆ I can understand the difference between simple, compound and complex sentences and can use all three.

Structural effects in sentences

Learning objective
Your will learn how to
- explore how different sentences can be used to create special effects in writing.

Assessment objectives
- English Language AO2, AO6
- English Literature AO2

Does it make any difference what types of sentence you use?

Getting you thinking

You've discovered already that sentences can be structured in different ways.

These structures can create special effects within a text.

 Look at the following two sentences from a novel by Jon McGregor, one of which is a **minor sentence**, the other a complex sentence.

> So listen.
>
> He traverses streets of dirty, straggling houses, with now and then an unexpected court composed of buildings as ill-proportioned and deformed as the half-naked children that wallow in the kennels.
>
> Jon McGregor, *If Nobody Speaks of Remarkable Things*

Key term

minor sentence: a sentence that lacks one or more of the elements that go to make up a full sentence, for example, a subject or a main verb

  a Which sentence gives you more detail and description?
  b Which one forces you to stop?
  c Which one has the slowest pace? How does it do this?
  d Which one creates the most drama and tension?
  e Which one creates the most visual image in your mind's eye?

Explore the skills

2. Read the following extract from the same novel by Jon McGregor where he describes a city at night. Explore how the writer has used unusual sentence structures for effect by answering the questions in the annotations.

So listen.

Listen, and there is more to hear.

The rattle of a dustbin lid knocked to the floor.

The scrawl and scratch of two hackle-raised cats.

The sudden thundercrash of bottles emptied into crates. **1** The slam-slam of car doors, the changing of gears, the hobbled clip-clop of a slow walk home. **2** The rippled roll of shutters pulled down on late-night cafes, a crackled voice crying street names for taxis, a loud scream that lingers and cracks into laughter, a bang that might just be an old car backfiring, a callbox calling out for an answer, a treeful of birds tricked into morning, a whistle and a shout and a broken glass, a blare of soft music and a blam of hard beats, a barking and yelling and singing and crying and it all swells up all the rumbles and crashes and bangings and slams, all the noise and the rush and the non-stop wonder of the song of the city you can hear if you listen the song **3**

and it stops **4**

in some rare and sacred dead time, sandwiched **5** between the late sleepers and the early risers, there is a miracle of silence. **6**

Everything has stopped. **7**

1 What is unusual about each of these three sentences? Do they have a subject?

2 Is this a sentence? What do you notice about the listing?

3 Is this a sentence? What effect is the writer trying to create through the use of **syndetic listing**?

4 Has the sentence finished yet? How does the structure here bring you up short? Does this change the pace?

5 What do you think is the importance of this word in relation to the structure of the sentence?

6 Look back at the whole sentence. Is it understandable in this context? How is additional impact created when the sentence stops? How does the sentence reflect the night itself?

7 What is the impact of the spacing and the simple sentence at the end? Why does this sentence become unusual in relation to the previous ones?

Key term

syndetic list: uses a conjunction, most commonly 'and', within its list of items; an asyndetic list does not

Develop the skills

Read the following extract from *Sketches by Boz* by Charles Dickens, where he describes an area of London, the Dials, in the 1800s. Use the advice on reading long complex sentences from 1.2 to help you. Then complete the activities below.

The peculiar character of these streets, and the close resemblance each one bears to its neighbour, by no means tends to decrease the bewilderment in which the unexperienced wayfarer through 'the Dials' finds himself involved. Here and there, a little dark chandler's shop, with a cracked bell hung up behind the door to announce the entrance of a customer, or betray the presence of some young gentleman in whom a passion for shop tills has developed itself at an early age: others, as if for support, against some handsome lofty building, which usurps the place of a low dingy public-house; long rows of broken and patched windows expose plants that may have flourished when 'the Dials' were built, in vessels as dirty as 'the Dials' themselves; and shops for the purchase of rags, bones, old iron, and kitchen-stuff, vie in cleanliness with the bird-fanciers and rabbit-dealers, which one might fancy so many arks, but for the irresistible conviction that no bird in its proper senses, who was permitted to leave one of them, would ever come back again. Brokers' shops, which would seem to have been established by humane individuals, as refuges for destitute bugs, interspersed with announcements of day-schools, penny theatres, petition-writers, mangles, and music for balls or routs, complete the 'still life' of the subject; and dirty men, filthy women, squalid children, fluttering shuttlecocks, noisy battledores, reeking pipes, bad fruit, more than doubtful oysters, attenuated cats, depressed dogs, and anatomical fowls, are its cheerful accompaniments.

Charles Dickens, from *Sketches by Boz*

3 The whole of the area highlighted in yellow is one sentence. Answer these questions about the sentence.

a What is the purpose of the 'cracked bell'?

b What is unusual about the arrangement of buildings in 'the Dials'?

c What different types of shops are in 'the Dials'?

d How many separate ideas related to the shops are included in the one sentence?

4 The whole of the area in blue is also one sentence. Now answer these questions.

  a Identify the main clause in this sentence.

  b What things does Dickens allow you to 'see' in the brokers' shops?

  c What kinds of people does Dickens allow you to 'meet' in the brokers' shops?

  d What is the effect of the listing in creating an image of the brokers' shops?

Both the McGregor extract and the Dickens extract describe aspects of a city. One was written in 2001, the other in 1836.

5 Identify the similarities in the way that both writers use sentences for effect. You might think about:

- complexity of sentences
- unusual forms of sentences
- patterns and listing
- creating a specific pace to match the topic.

Collect your ideas into a mind map and add quotations from both texts to show the similarities between the two.

Apply the skills

6 Write your own description of a particular aspect of a town or city. For example:

- a busy railway station or bus station
- a shopping precinct or market place
- a busy coffee shop.

Include some of the techniques that both Dickens and McGregor have used to good effect such as:

- highly complex sentence structures
- minor sentences
- patterns and listing.

7 Now pull together all your findings on sentence structure to undertake the following task.

Write a short commentary in 200–300 words exploring how your choices of sentence structures add to the meaning and impact of the description.

Checklist for success

- Identify the different sentence functions, clauses and phrases.
- Give clear examples.
- Explain in detail how they might add to the purpose, the meaning and the impact of the text on its audience.

Check your progress:

I can interpret the meanings and effects of a text by deconstructing and commenting on its sentences, phrases, and clauses as well as using those varied structures for effect in my own writing.

I can understand that using different sentence structures adds to the meaning and impact of a text for the reader or audience.

I can see that using different sentence structures creates different moods or feelings within a text.

Check your progress

- I can recognise different types of phrases and use them to work out the precise inferences and effects that a writer creates, as well as apply them in my own work to produce specific effects.

- I can understand how to decode the most complex sentences to extract key meanings and how to use different sentence types to create precise meanings in my own work.

- I can interpret the meanings and effects of a text by deconstructing and commenting on its sentences, phrases, and clauses as well as using those varied structures for effect in my own writing.

- I can recognise different types of phrases in texts and comment on their use as well as include a variety of them in my own writing.

- I can understand how each sentence type is constructed and how to use them in my own work for effect.

- I can understand that using different sentence structures adds to the meaning and impact of a text for the reader or audience.

- I can identify the names of different types of phrases and use some of them in my writing.

- I can understand the difference between simple, compound and complex sentences and can use all three.

- I can see that using different sentence structures creates different moods or feelings within a text.

Chapter 2

Key concepts

What's it all about?

What is it that gives each text its own individual flavour and yet also makes it familiar or fit our expectations? By exploring these questions, this chapter introduces some of the key concepts that you will need for GCSE study. You will examine how texts can be interpreted in different ways, you will consider the ways in which a genre of writing has developed and been subverted over time, and how writers make a narrative voice unique and convincing. Your understanding of these key concepts will help you in your own writing and analysis of texts.

In this chapter, you will learn how to

- explore meanings and interpretations
- explore the conventions of genre
- explore narrative voices.

	English Language GCSE	English Literature GCSE
How will this be tested?	In your exam, you will be expected to read and understand some previously unseen sources. You will be expected to explain the ideas in them. You will also be asked to think about the ways in which they have been written, including the words that have been used and the ways in which the sources have been structured and organised. You will also have the opportunity to apply your understanding of genre and narrative voice in your own creative and discursive writing.	In your exam, you will be asked to develop your own interpretation of texts and analyse the ways in which writers communicate their ideas and viewpoints to the reader. You will write about a range of different genres. You will be expected to consider the range of ways a writer has communicated their ideas, including the language they use, the literary techniques they employ, and the ways in which the text is structured and organised.

Explore meanings and interpretations

Learning objectives
You will learn how to
- explore meaning in a range of ways
- comment on how writers interpret similar ideas differently.

Assessment objective
- English Language AO1

What does 'interpreting' a text mean?

Getting you thinking

Look at these two images.

1. **a** In what way could the two pictures be said to be 'about the same thing'?

    b In what way could the two pictures be said to be different?

Explore the skills

When you are studying a writer's work you will often be asked to 'analyse' or 'explore'. Much of this is to enable you to get at an **interpretation** of a text. But interpretation is a troublesome concept for both writers *and* readers.

Your response to a text is like a meeting point between you, the text and the writer.

Key term

interpretation: a particular way of looking at or understanding something

You	*Your response*	*The text*
Knowledge	Your exploration of the text	The language choices and their effects
Experiences	Your interpretation of the text	The form and structure and their effects
Feelings		The writer's ideas or viewpoint
Other things you have read or seen		

Through *exploration* of the text, you learn to read *critically*.

Exploration means:

- finding your way around something
- discovering or finding out more about it
- going down new or unexpected routes
- inspecting things in detail which interest you.

Reading *critically* means:

- asking questions
- considering different interpretations (ways of making sense of what you have encountered)
- reflecting on your discoveries and drawing conclusions.

2 Look at the picture on the right of page 22. It is Van Gogh's *The Starry Night*. Explore this painting. Make notes using the questions below:

    a What do you see first, from a distance? (For example, *A night sky with stars*.)

    b Look closer. What do you notice about the stars and their appearance? What shape are they? What do they seem to be doing? Is there anything unexpected in how Van Gogh has painted them?

    c What thoughts, feelings or experiences has Van Gogh expressed in his depiction?

    d Reflect on your thoughts – are the stars in the painting like the ones you have seen?

Develop the skills

An important fact about language is that it is open to different interpretations.

3 Think about a phrase such as 'bright star'. List all the possible **synonyms** for, and **connotations** of, the word 'bright'. These can be both literal and metaphorical meanings. Here are a couple to start you off: *sunny, shining.*

4 Now list as many connotations and synonyms you can think of for 'star'. Again, these can be both literal and metaphorical meanings.

5 In 2009, a film called *Bright Star* was released about the poet John Keats. Write a sentence explaining why this might be a good title for the film.

The **plurality** of meaning is a useful idea to keep in mind when exploring texts, particularly challenging ones. This does not mean that *any* interpretation is acceptable. But it does mean there might be a range of meanings, or interpretations, which you can test out as a critical reader.

6 Write a paragraph about the Van Gogh painting, explaining your own interpretation of it. Go back to your 'explore' questions if you need to.

Key terms

synonyms: words or phrases with identical or very close meanings

connotations: ideas, images or associations brought to mind by a word or phrase

plurality: more than one, but not infinite

Now read the following poem by T.S. Eliot.

Virginia

Red river, red river,
Slow flow heat is silence
No will is still as a river
Still. Will heat move
Only through the mocking-bird
Heard once? Still hills
Wait. Gates wait. Purple trees,
White trees, wait, wait,
Delay, decay. Living, living,
Never moving. Ever moving
Iron thoughts came with me
And go with me:
Red river river river.

T.S. Eliot

Poets often use and organise language in unusual ways in order to convey powerful ideas or create memorable images.

7 What is unusual or challenging about this poem?

8 What methods could you use to arrive at an interpretation of the poem?

When faced with a difficult text, such as Eliot's poem, your exploration should follow the same path as the one you took in exploring Van Gogh's painting.

Start with the simple things: what is obvious? What is happening in the poem?

> The poet is describing a river and the surrounding landscape.

Move on to a deeper exploration:

* What stands out or is noticeable in the poem?
* Do any particular words, phrases or lines seem particularly powerful?
* What questions are raised by these words or phrases?
* Can you think of possible answers?
* What connotations or ideas come to mind from particular words or phrases?

Read this student's exploration of the first four lines:

Red river, red river,————— repeated noun phrase – rhythmic, blood?
Slow flow heat is silence——— river moves slowly
No will is still as a river———— is this phrase separate? Or is the 'heat' flowing slowly?
Still. Will heat move————— means 'not moving' but also 'always'

9 Using a copy of the poem, do the same type of exploration for the remaining lines. Remember to focus not just on understanding or meaning, but on raising questions, such as 'Why has Eliot allowed so many lines to run into each other?'. Use the guidance in the bullet points above.

Now read the following responses by two students to the beginning and the ending of the poem.

Student A

The river is red, which means danger, so it is a dangerous river. This means that the writer must have had an accident or problem with the river as a child. Because it says 'red river' twice, it means there are two rivers. They must be next to each other.

Student B

The poem begins with a description of the river, with the same repeated refrain — 'red river, red river' — and ends with a similar description, this time with the word 'river' repeated three times. This repetitive phrasing suggests the constant flow of the water, and in the use of the word 'red', the pulse of your bloodstream. There is also a suggestion that the river is tidal in its ebb and flow.

10 Which of these two responses best describes what the poet does, makes connections and explores interpretations by suggesting several solutions?

11 In what ways does this response do this?

12 Do you agree with this student's interpretations?

Apply the skills

13 Now pull together all of your findings to undertake the following task.

Write 200–250 words about 'Virginia' focusing on how the narrator seems to feel about the river. Ensure you explore the poem fully, raising questions and suggesting your own interpretation or answers.

Checklist for success

- Support what you say with evidence, otherwise your response will simply be an **assertion**.
- Look to link the text with your response – what has Eliot done or expressed and how do you respond to it?
- Consider a range of interpretations and possibilities.

Key term

assertion: a statement presented as fact but without evidence

Check your progress:

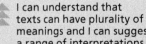 I can understand that texts can have plurality of meanings and I can suggest a range of interpretations supported by evidence.

I can raise questions about challenging texts, and suggest some of my own answers or interpretations.

I can explore and explain possible meanings in texts.

Explore the conventions of genre

Learning objectives
You will learn how to
• comment on genre conventions
• recognise and comment on how writers challenge or play with these conventions.

Assessment objectives
• English Language AO1
• English Literature AO1

What are conventions and how do writers use them in different ways?

Getting you thinking

Writers engage readers by producing what they want or expect, but also by doing the unexpected: for example, by taking a well-known style of story and making us look at it in new ways.

One well-known **genre** is gothic fiction. It emerged in the seventeenth and eighteenth centuries and became incredibly popular.

1 The following table contains many of gothic fiction's **conventions** and it also lists two other well-known genres from the present day. Copy and complete the table.

Key terms

genre: category or type of text, such as 'detective' or 'chick lit'

conventions: recognisable or accepted features of a particular genre

Genre	Gothic	Sci-fi	Teen romance
Location/ settings	Castles, churches, ruins, forests		
Typical characters	Beautiful young heroine (often in danger, sometimes orphaned); villainous, usually older man (often a relative, aristocrat); priests, monks		
Typical plot or themes	Curiosity (on part of main character to uncover mystery); desire; greed; cruelty; murder; elements of supernatural; imprisonment		
Typical language	Exaggerated and emotive speech; highly-descriptive settings		
Other	Key objects: cloaks, daggers, candle		

Explore the skills

The following extract comes from one of the very first gothic tales.

Manfred is Lord of Otranto. His son has been crushed to death on his wedding day by a huge falling helmet. Manfred demands to see Isabella, his son's beautiful fiancée, in order to make a shocking proposal.

> 'I tell you,' said Manfred imperiously, 'Hippolita is no longer my wife; I divorce her from this hour. Too long has she cursed me by her unfruitfulness. My fate depends on having sons, and this night I trust will give a new date to my hopes.'
>
> At those words he seized the cold hand of Isabella, who was half dead with fright and horror. She shrieked, and started from him, Manfred rose to pursue her, when the moon, which was now up, and gleamed in at the opposite casement, presented to his sight the plumes of the fatal helmet, which rose to the height of the windows, waving backwards and forwards in a tempestuous manner, and accompanied with a hollow and rustling sound. Isabella, who gathered courage from her situation, and who dreaded nothing so much as Manfred's pursuit of his declaration, cried—
>
> 'Look, my Lord! see, Heaven itself declares against your impious intentions!'
>
> 'Heaven nor Hell shall impede my designs,' said Manfred, advancing again to seize the Princess.
>
> Horace Walpole, from *The Castle of Otranto*

2   Which conventions of gothic fiction can you identify here? Make notes on:
- the characters and their behaviour
- the setting and weather
- clues about the plot or themes
- the style of language (for example, the use of particular verbs or the kind of dialogue).

3   Gothic fiction depends on the creation of a powerful atmosphere or mood. Write one to two sentences explaining what sort of atmosphere is created in the extract above.

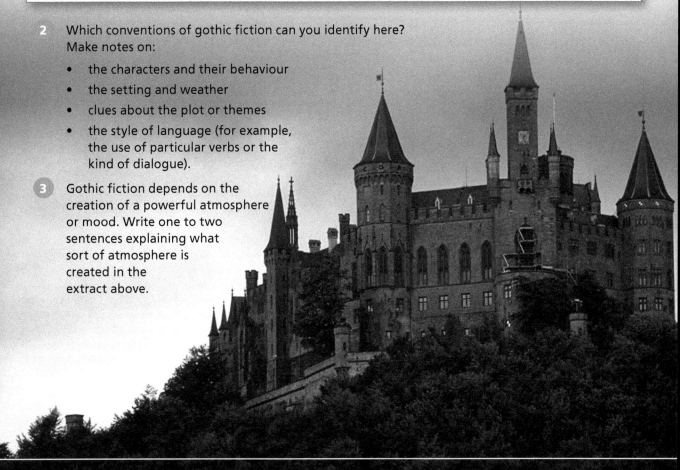

Develop the skills

Gothic fiction was criticised at the time for being both too realistic (it dealt with emotions and actions which were normally repressed) and, in contrast, too unlikely (it had fairy tale settings, with unreal characters). In this context, Jane Austen, known for her social novels such as *Pride and Prejudice*, wrote *Northanger Abbey*. The title suggested it was another gothic novel, with its reference to an old building, and the word 'anger' hidden in its name.

Read the opening, and compare it to Walpole's.

> No one who had ever seen Catherine Morland in her infancy would have supposed her born to be an heroine. Her situation in life, the character of her father and mother, her own person and disposition, were all equally against her. Her father was a clergyman, without being neglected, or poor, and a very respectable man, though his name was Richard – and he had never been handsome. He had a considerable independence besides two good livings – and he was not in the least addicted to locking up his daughters. Her mother was a woman of useful plain sense, with a good temper, and, what is more remarkable, with a good constitution. She had three sons before Catherine was born; and instead of dying in bringing the latter into the world, as anybody might expect, she still lived on – lived to have six children more – to see them growing up around her, and to enjoy excellent health herself. A family of ten children will be always called a fine family, where there are heads and arms and legs enough for the number; but the Morlands had little other right to the word, for they were in general very plain, and Catherine, for many years of her life, as plain as any. She had a thin awkward figure, a sallow skin without colour, dark lank hair, and strong features – so much for her person; and not less unpropitious for heroism seemed her mind. She was fond of all boys' plays, and greatly preferred cricket not merely to dolls, but to the more heroic enjoyments of infancy, nursing a dormouse, feeding a canary-bird, or watering a rose-bush.
>
> Jane Austen, from *Northanger Abbey*

4 Write answers to these questions:

   a Does this sound like the opening to a gothic novel?

   b Does Catherine sound like a typical gothic heroine? Why? Why not?

   c Does this sound like a typical gothic setting or background?

   d How does the mood or atmosphere contrast with that in the extract from *The Castle of Otranto*?

5 Write a paragraph about what you think Austen's purpose might be here, answering the following questions:

   a What is the effect of her choices?

   b Is she mocking the gothic genre or trying to tell a realistic story? Or both?

Apply the skills

6 The following task considers a text from the twentieth century that shows how writers have continued to draw on elements of the gothic in more recent times.

In this famous opening passage of the novel *Rebecca* by Daphne du Maurier, the central character dreams of returning to her former home, 'Manderley' – a huge, imposing house full of dark secrets.

Last night I dreamt I went to Manderley again. It seemed to me I stood by the iron gate leading to the drive, and for a while I could not enter, for the way was barred to me. There was a padlock and chain upon the gate. I called in my dream to the lodge-keeper, and had no answer, and peering closer through the rusted spokes of the gate I saw that the lodge was uninhabited. No smoke came from the chimney, and the little lattice windows gaped forlorn. Then, like all dreamers, I was possessed of a sudden with supernatural powers and passed like a spirit through the barrier before me. The drive wound away in front of me, twisting and turning as it had always done, but as I advanced I was aware that a change had come upon it; it was narrow and unkempt, not the drive that we had known. At first I was puzzled and did not understand, and it was only when I bent my head to avoid the low swinging branch of a tree that I realized what had happened. Nature had come into her own again and, little by little, in her stealthy, insidious way had encroached upon the drive with long, tenacious fingers. The woods, always a menace even in the past, had triumphed in the end. They crowded, dark and uncontrolled, to the borders of the drive. The beeches with white, naked limbs leant close to one another, their branches intermingled in a strange embrace, making a vault above my head like the archway of a church. And there were other trees as well, trees that I did not recognize, squat oaks and tortured elms that straggled cheek by jowl with the beeches, and had thrust themselves out of the quiet earth, along with monster shrubs and plants, none of which I remembered.

Daphne du Maurier, from *Rebecca*

How does the writer use elements of the gothic to create a sense of mystery and tension in this extract?

Checklist for success

- Write about the thoughts and feelings of the narrator.
- Explore how description of setting has been used to establish atmosphere.
- Select particular images and word choices that create the story's mood.

Check your progress:

I can analyse in precise detail how writers use and adapt particular conventions for effect.

I can identify the main conventions of literary genres and make some detailed comments on their use and impact.

I can explain clearly how writers use conventions and some of the effects created.

Explore narrative voices

How do writers create interesting narrative voices?

Getting you thinking

Read this opening to a story.

Text A

> Of course, I know that she loves me, and I love her. Ignoring me as I pass her in the corridor; not responding to my texts; going out with that tall blond guy in the sixth-form just to make me jealous. It's classic, isn't it? She knows I'm watching her, following her, making sure that no one hurts her. And if I was in any doubt, as I sit here on my bed, I see that she's just 'unfriended' me on Facebook. That's the clincher. She trusts me, and that's why we don't need to speak. It's our secret, our hidden love.

1. What is the narrator's view of the situation?

2. What do we see as readers?

3. What particular words, phrases or details give us a different **narrative perspective** from that of the narrator?

Explore the skills

Part of the pleasure of reading comes from being taken into someone else's world. Narrative voice is a key part of this process.

A common type of narrative voice today is the **first person**, although this was less common in nineteenth-century fiction. In many short stories or novels, it is this narrator whose experiences we follow, as if looking at the world through their eyes. But 'narrate' means to 'tell a story'. Can you trust your narrator to tell the whole truth?

Key terms

narrative perspective: in this extract, the narrative perspective comes from the language used, for example, there are many pronouns and possessives – *I, her, she, our* and *us* – which focus on the relationship

first person: mode of narrating which uses 'I' to tell the story

4. What other language choices does the writer of Text A make? Make notes under these questions:

   a What tense is mainly used? What is its effect?

   b The writer uses participles such as 'ignoring'; can you find any others? What is the effect of having these so close together?

   c What overall impression do we get of the narrator as a result?

The particular style of narrative voice can also be altered quite significantly.

Here is the same opening told in a different way:

Text B

> Her flowing hair. Her golden skin. Goddess. I worship her, an acolyte, from afar, but I am the one true believer, and only I am worthy. The rain batters the windows in the corridor as I watch her. Her eyes are averted. But she sees me anyway. An emotional current flows. Electric. Electra.

5. What are the key differences in style and tone here between the first opening and this one? Think about:

   • the type of sentences and use of grammar

   • the vocabulary and how information is conveyed

   • any **analogies** or **allusions.**

   What different impression does this give us of the narrator?

Now read this alternative opening to the same story.

Key terms

analogies: extended comparisons made between two ideas or experiences

allusions: references to other stories or texts

Text C

> Mollie knew that the small, wiry kid in Year 10 was obsessed with her. She had seen him creeping around at school, peeking at her from a distance, and somehow he had got hold of her mobile number. At first, she'd tolerated it – even accepted him as a friend on Facebook. However, when he started commenting on her photos that was the last straw. Her boyfriend Ben was clear about it: 'Unfriend him!' So, she did, almost without a thought, as they stood at the bus stop that evening.

6. Whose perspective is this? How do you know?

7   How do the choices of words and phrases in each text suggest
     different perspectives and points of view? Copy and complete
     this table.

Text A	Text C	Perspectives?
'love her'	'obsessed with her'	Narrator in Text A sees it as romantic attachment; Mollie in Text C sees it as unhealthy
'following her'	'creeping around'	
'that tall blond guy'	'boyfriend Ben'	
'the clincher'	'the last straw'	
'on my bed'	'at the bus stop'	

8   Write a further paragraph in which the boy watches Mollie
     from outside her house. You must:

     •   write either from his or her point of view

     •   maintain a similar perspective and narrative style if you
         write as Mollie

     •   decide either to use the first or second example from the
         boy's perspective and keep to that style.

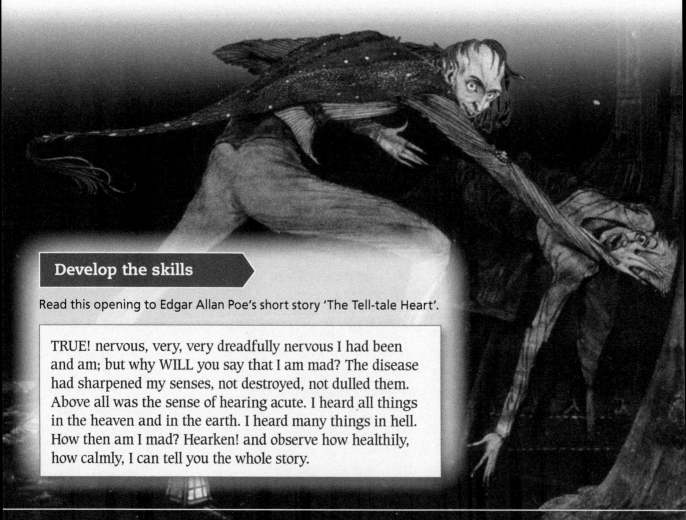

Develop the skills

Read this opening to Edgar Allan Poe's short story 'The Tell-tale Heart'.

TRUE! nervous, very, very dreadfully nervous I had been
and am; but why WILL you say that I am mad? The disease
had sharpened my senses, not destroyed, not dulled them.
Above all was the sense of hearing acute. I heard all things
in the heaven and in the earth. I heard many things in hell.
How then am I mad? Hearken! and observe how healthily,
how calmly, I can tell you the whole story.

> It is impossible to say how first the idea entered my brain, but, once conceived, it haunted me day and night. Object there was none. Passion there was none. I loved the old man. He had never wronged me. He had never given me insult. For his gold I had no desire. I think it was his eye! Yes, it was this! One of his eyes resembled that of a vulture – a pale blue eye with a film over it. Whenever it fell upon me my blood ran cold, and so by degrees, very gradually, I made up my mind to take the life of the old man, and thus rid myself of the eye for ever.
>
> Edgar Allan Poe, from 'The Tell-tale Heart'

9   Write two paragraphs about the narrative voice used here. Do you trust this narrator?

- In the first, comment on the narrator and his perspective, for example, the unreliability of what we are told: how *what he says* is rather **ironic** given the *way he says it.*

- In the second, comment on the narrative style – the choice of vocabulary; the use of punctuation; the style of sentences; the form of **address**.

Apply the skills

10   In the following task, try out the ideas on narrative voice in your own writing.

Write the opening three paragraphs to a story with the title 'Obsession'. Before you begin, draft some ideas about the story and the main character, or **protagonist**, for example:

- who he or she is

- what the subject or topic of obsession is

- what the problem or obstacle is that the main character faces or must overcome.

Checklist for success

- Decide on a particular perspective and maintain it throughout the opening.

- Select language and grammar that conveys the particular tone of voice you require (for example, lots of sharp, short questions to suggest someone irrational or unstable).

- Decide whether your reader will trust this narrator.

Key terms

ironic: pointing out the difference between the surface and the reality of a situation

address: the mode of speaking to the reader (for example, direct, distant, objective)

Key term

protagonist: the main character in a story whose behaviour we follow as readers

Check your progress:

 I can comment on the effects of a range of narrative voices and perspectives, and am able to apply this to convey a particular and convincing tone in my own writing.

 I can recognise the differences between narrative voices and perspectives, and try out some of them in my own writing.

I can identify some different narrative perspectives, and write an opening which maintains one perspective.

Check your progress

- I understand that texts can have plurality of meanings and I can suggest a range of interpretations supported by evidence.

- I can analyse in detail how writers use and adapt particular conventions for effect.

- I can comment on the effects of a range of narrative voices and perspectives, and am able to apply this to convey a particular and convincing tone in my own writing.

- I can raise questions about challenging texts, and suggest some of my own answers or interpretations.

- I can identify the main conventions of literary genres and make some detailed comments on their use and impact.

- I can recognise the differences between narrative voices and perspectives, and apply some of them in my own writing.

- I can explore and explain possible meanings in texts.

- I can explain clearly how writers use conventions and some of the effects created.

- I can identify some different narrative perspectives, and write an opening which maintains one perspective.

Chapter 3

Reading, understanding and responding to texts

What's it all about?

In this chapter, you will tackle a range of challenging texts and explore a number of techniques for breaking them down, for example, dealing with difficulties in understanding complex ideas or unfamiliar vocabulary. You will also explore how you can approach two texts with similar subject matter but written from differing perspectives or contexts, in order to synthesise key ideas or concepts.

In this chapter, you will learn how to

- understand more challenging texts
- use textual support in sophisticated ways
- synthesise and summarise more challenging texts
- apply your skills to English Language and English Literature tasks.

	English Language GCSE	English Literature GCSE
Which AOs are covered?	**AO1** Identify and interpret explicit and implicit information and ideas Select and synthesise evidence from different texts **AO4** Evaluate texts critically and support this with appropriate textual references	**AO1** Read, understand and respond to texts. Students should be able to: • maintain a critical style and develop an informed personal response • use textual references, including quotations, to support and illustrate interpretations
How will this be tested?	Questions will require you to apply what you have learned about how to approach challenging texts, and comment on them in an informed and insightful way. You will need to demonstrate that you can select apt evidence and use it selectively and appropriately.	Questions will require you to draw on evidence selectively and appropriately, and write in a fluent manner showing insight and sustained understanding of both explicit and implicit ideas.

Understand more challenging texts

Learning objective
You will learn how to
- tackle the comprehension of more complex texts.

Assessment objectives
- English Language AO1, AO4
- English Literature AO1

What techniques can you use to make sense of difficult texts?

Getting you thinking

Some of the main reasons why texts are challenging are that they:

- use unfamiliar vocabulary
- use unfamiliar or complex sentence structures
- refer to unfamiliar concepts or things that are outside your own experiences.

1 Look at the following extract from an autobiography.

> In the latter part of my school life I became passionately fond of shooting

What possible meanings might you be able to infer from this extract?

2 What kind of person might have written this autobiography:

- a famous gangster
- someone with a deep interest in nature and wildlife
- an aristocrat with a country estate?

Explore the skills

Unfamiliar vocabulary can be unsettling, particularly in unseen texts. Instead of worrying about the unfamiliar, try to focus on the familiar, where the real clues to meaning might lie.

The following box contains a number of unfamiliar words and some phrases that we don't often use in the same way now.

gentleman	White's 'Selborne'	Cicindela
took much pleasure	simplicity	much zeal
(Zygaena)	*named* mineral	Hemipterous
some little care	very much	with respect to

3 Read the following extract from the autobiography of the famous naturalist Charles Darwin.

Without worrying about the missing words, decide on what you learn about Darwin as a boy from the text. Then write a short paragraph in clear statement sentences presenting your thoughts.

> ………….. science, I continued collecting minerals with …………, but quite unscientifically—all that I cared about was a new ……, and I hardly attempted to classify them. I must have observed insects with ……, for when ten years old (1819) I went for three weeks to Plas Edwards on the sea-coast in Wales, I was …… interested and surprised at seeing a large black and scarlet ……… insect, many moths ……. , and a ……. which are not found in Shropshire. I almost made up my mind to begin collecting all the insects which I could find dead, for on consulting my sister I concluded that it was not right to kill insects for the sake of making a collection. From reading ………, I …….. in watching the habits of birds, and even made notes on the subject. In my ……… I remember wondering why every …….. did not become an ornithologist.
>
> Adapted from Charles Darwin, *The Autobiography of Charles Darwin*

4 Look back at the box of unfamiliar words and phrases. Decide which word or phrase fits into each of the spaces above. Make a copy of the passage with them in place.

5 Now look at the paragraph you wrote about Charles Darwin as a boy. Are your statements still valid?

The chances are that all of the basic meaning you were able to infer from the text has come from the vocabulary that was most familiar to you. The key message is not to be distracted by unfamiliar words, but to work logically with what you *do* know.

Try this technique for yourself by reading the next sentence from Darwin's autobiography and then using it to add any extra points to your paragraph about Darwin as a boy.

> Early in my school days a boy had a copy of the 'Wonders of the World', which I often read, and disputed with other boys about the veracity of some of the statements; and I believe that this book first gave me a wish to travel in remote countries, which was ultimately fulfilled by the voyage of the *Beagle*.

Develop the skills

In dealing with unfamiliar concepts, it is important to use your powers of questioning. Treat the text like a puzzle and use some 'stop and think' questioning techniques to help you.

You will understand more than you think, once you do some **inferential reading**.

Key term

inferential reading: reading beyond the surface or literal meaning by considering what is implied or suggested by a text

 Look at the following task.

> What do you understand about Charles Darwin's favourite hobby as an older boy?

Use a student's 'stop and think' questions in the annotations below to help you understand the text, then answer the task in a short paragraph.

> In the latter part of my school life I became passionately fond of shooting; I do not believe that any one could have shown more zeal for the most holy cause than I did for shooting birds. How well I remember killing my first snipe, and my excitement was so great that I had much difficulty in reloading my gun from the trembling of my hands. This taste long continued, and I became a very good shot. When at Cambridge I used to practise throwing up my gun to my shoulder before a looking-glass to see that I threw it up straight. Another and better plan was to get a friend to wave about a lighted candle, and then to fire at it with a cap on the nipple, and if the aim was accurate the little puff of air would blow out the candle. The explosion of the cap caused a sharp crack, and I was told that the tutor of the college remarked, "What an extraordinary thing it is, Mr. Darwin seems to spend hours in cracking a horse-whip in his room, for I often hear the crack when I pass under his windows."

Shooting? Does he mean criminal or sporting?

In that case, what sort of 'sport'? Who does that?

What's a snipe? I need to look back to the previous sentence for a clue.

The town or the university – what do I think?

Why is he doing this here? Doesn't he have a party to go to? What image have I got of him?

He's doing what?! Isn't this dangerous? Does this add to the image of the time?

Why does the tutor call him that? And who has a horse-whip anyway? Does this also give a picture of the time?

Dealing with unfamiliar syntax and sentence structures can also be a challenge. Aim to break down lengthy sentences into their key ideas.

Remind yourself of the advice in 1.2 about how to unpack complex sentences.

8 Look at this final extract from Darwin's autobiography and make a list in note form of the key idea or ideas in each of the sentences in your own words. Remember to use your techniques from Activities 4 and 7 to deal with unfamiliar vocabulary and structures. The sentences have been numbered to help you.

Towards the close of my school life, my brother worked hard at chemistry, and made a fair laboratory with proper apparatus in the tool-house in the garden, and I was allowed to aid him as a servant in most of his experiments. **1** He made all the gases and many compounds, and I read with great care several books on chemistry, such as Henry and Parkes' 'Chemical Catechism.' **2** The subject interested me greatly, and we often used to go on working till rather late at night. **3** This was the best part of my education at school, for it showed me practically the meaning of experimental science. **4** The fact that we worked at chemistry somehow got known at school, and as it was an unprecedented fact, I was nicknamed 'Gas.' **5** I was also once publicly rebuked by the head-master, Dr. Butler, for thus wasting my time on such useless subjects; and he called me very unjustly a 'poco curante,' and as I did not understand what he meant, it seemed to me a fearful reproach. **6**

Apply the skills

9 Now use all three extracts and the information and understanding you have gained from Activities 3 to 8 to answer the following task.

What do we understand about Charles Darwin when he was young from the extracts taken from his autobiography?

Checklist for success

* Make clear statements in your own words, addressing the question directly.
* Support these statements with selected quotations.
* Use inferences to show your understanding.

Check your progress:

▲▲ I can read and understand more challenging texts, selecting information and showing a perceptive understanding.

▲▲ I can read more challenging texts, selecting information and clearly showing my understanding.

▲ I can read unfamiliar texts, selecting information and clearly showing my understanding.

Use textual support in sophisticated ways

Learning objective
You will learn how to
* use the textual support in more sophisticated ways.

Assessment objectives
* English Language AO1, AO4
* English Literature AO1

How can you use the text more effectively to back up your ideas?

Getting you thinking

A student has been planning and writing an answer on the following task.

How does Lord Byron present both inner and outer beauty in the poem 'She Walks in Beauty'?

She Walks in Beauty

She walks in beauty, like the night
  Of cloudless climes and starry skies;
And all that's best of dark and bright
  Meet in her aspect and her eyes;
Thus mellowed to that tender light
  Which heaven to gaudy day denies.

One shade the more, one ray the less,
  Had half impaired the nameless grace
Which waves in every raven tress,
  Or softly lightens o'er her face;
Where thoughts serenely sweet express,
  How pure, how dear their dwelling-place.

And on that cheek, and o'er that brow,
  So soft, so calm, yet eloquent,
The smiles that win, the tints that glow,
  But tell of days in goodness spent,
A mind at peace with all below,
  A heart whose love is innocent!

Lord Byron

1 Read this extract from the student's response to the task.

   a What method are they using to present their idea?

   b How have they used quotation?

> Lord Byron presents an image of a stunningly beautiful woman:
> 'She walks in beauty like the night / Of cloudless climes and
> starry skies'. This suggests that she is as beautiful as the
> heavens above on a beautiful, clear night.

Explore the skills

The student has used quotation to support their idea and made a useful inference. However, in order to present a more sophisticated argument, you can present your evidence in more subtle ways than just copying out a line or two of the text.

You could:
- **embed** quotations within your answer
- use a quotation as a **starting point** to present an idea
- use **close textual reference** instead of a direct quotation.

2 In the table below, there are a number of ideas about Byron's poem that the student has planned to write about. However, the ideas need support from the text. Make a copy of the table, adding in any further ideas from your own reading of the poem.

Ideas about outer beauty	Ideas about inner beauty
Idea of her moving 'in' beauty – it's like a bubble surrounding her – she's got a sort of aura	Talks about her eyes but also her facial expression is mellow and calm. Seems like a good person
Compares her to the beauty of darkness – not like usual – women often described as 'fair' back then	He mentions words like grace – suggests she has something natural about her – not just her looks but her manner
It's like daylight is too bright and brash – too dazzling – may be like other women he has met	Lots of words like soft and serene and calm. Like she's an angel
Light and shade in her hair. Her hair is dark also	

Using embedded quotation means that you select words from the poem and integrate them into your own sentences to support the point you are making. The final sentence will make sense in its own right, seamlessly blending your ideas and your quotations.

Look at this example of the use of embedded quotation considering Byron's presentation of *outer* beauty.

> Byron's subject has an aura of beauty around her in the same way that the night sky offers us 'all that's best of dark and bright'. She epitomises the beauty of the darkness when it is lit by 'starry skies' and he challenges the accepted notions of what beauty is, when it is often linked with fairness.

3 Take one of the ideas considering Byron's presentation of *inner* beauty and write one or two sentences where you embed quotations from the text.

Develop the skills

A further way of supporting your ideas is to present your chosen quotation as a **starting point** for exploration to show the development of your ideas. Separate aspects of the quotation can then be 'zoomed' in on, for closer analysis.

4 Look at this quotation and the ideas it opens up in the annotations. Note how the two separate lines have been indicated.

> Thus mellowed **1** to that tender light **2** /Which heaven **3** to gaudy day **4** denies **5**

1 suggests mellow light but also her mellow nature – calmness

2 sounds gentle and beautiful, fragile even

3 something divine and also powerful

4 daylight is too brash and bright and dazzling – ostentatious – like other women

5 the daytime is denied the beautiful light of the night – making it more rare, precious, desirable

5 Select a quotation of your own from the poem to annotate as a **starting point** for further ideas.

Read this example response from the ideas gathered above and note how it 'zooms in' on details.

> 'Thus mellowed to that tender light/Which heaven to gaudy day denies' is how Byron concludes his initial perception of the woman. Her tranquil nature is reflected in the 'mellowed' nature of the 'tender light', which sounds gentle, even fragile and is a metaphor for her rare beauty. The beautiful light of the night is one that is 'denied' to the daytime by the all-powerful 'heavens' again making it rare, precious and desirable – as the woman appears to Byron. By contrast, 'gaudy day' is too brash and showy, too bright and dazzling and Byron here suggests the ostentatiousness of other women compared to this one.

6 Write up your own ideas from Activity 5, using your quotation as the **starting point**, and your 'zoom lens' on key details.

Using **close textual references** from a text, rather than quotations, is another sophisticated strategy for supporting ideas.

This can be particularly useful if you are dealing with a longer text such as a play or a novel. A textual reference is where you might refer to a precise detail, moment, or specific event to back up a point you are making. It is just as valid in showing your knowledge of the text as a direct quotation.

7 Look at the following example and decide which particular lines of the text are being discussed.

> Byron refers to the oppositional forces of darkness and light that play within the woman's hair, and provide a contrast to her skin. Again the darkness is gentle and the movement of her hair as she walks conveys something almost beyond description.

8 *Without looking back at the poem*, write up two to three sentences of your text explaining how the woman's face gave Byron a sense of her inner beauty. Refer to details in the text without using quotations at all.

Apply the skills

9 Read the sonnet by William Shakespeare before undertaking the following task.

> How does Shakespeare present both inner and outer beauty in the sonnet?
>
> Gather two or three ideas about inner beauty and outer beauty in a table like the example in Activity 2. Write up each idea in two or three sentences.

Sonnet 130

My mistress' eyes are nothing like the sun;
Coral is far more red than her lips' red;
If snow be white, why then her breasts are dun;
If hairs be wires, black wires grow on her head.
I have seen roses damasked, red and white,
But no such roses see I in her cheeks;
And in some perfumes is there more delight
Than in the breath that from my mistress reeks.
I love to hear her speak, yet well I know
That music hath a far more pleasing sound;
I grant I never saw a goddess go;
My mistress when she walks treads on the ground.
    And yet, by heaven, I think my love as rare
    As any she belied with false compare.

William Shakespeare

Check your progress:

- ▲▲▲ I can select and use a range of quotations and/or close textual references in a sophisticated way.
- ▲▲ I can select and use relevant quotations and/or close textual references.
- ▲ I can choose my quotations carefully to support my points.

Checklist for success

- Embed quotations in your sentences.
- Include quotations as a starting point for exploring ideas.
- Use close textual references.

Synthesise and summarise more challenging texts

Learning objective
You will learn how to
• use comprehension skills to understand and comment on more than one text in a fluent and informed way.
Assessment objectives
• English Language AO1
• English Literature AO1

How can you draw together ideas from two related texts in a clear and fluent way?

Getting you thinking

1 Read this extract from *The New York Times*.

Text A

> You need to see London at night, particularly the theaters. But not just the night life. London itself looks best in the dark. It's a pretty safe city, and you can walk in most places after sunset. It has a sedate and ghostly beauty. In the crepuscular kindness, you can see not just how she is, but how she once was, the layers of lives that have been lived here. Somebody with nothing better to do worked out that for every one of us living today, there are 15 ghosts. In most places you don't notice them, but in London you do. The dead and the fictional ghosts of Sherlock Holmes and Falstaff, Oliver Twist, Wendy and the Lost Boys, all the kindly, garrulous ghosts that accompany you in the night. The river runs like dark silk through the heart of the city, and the bridges dance with light. There are corners of silence in the revelry of the West End and Soho, and in the inky shadows foxes and owls patrol Hyde Park, which is still illuminated by gaslight.
>
> A.A. Gill, from 'My London, and Welcome to it', *The New York Times*, 27 April 2012

When working with a pair of challenging texts, it is helpful to begin with the most familiar or most contemporary text. This gives you a starting point for working with the second text.

2 Look at the following comprehension task, then collect ideas and evidence to answer it in a grid similar to the one below.

What do you learn about the atmosphere in London from Text A?

In Text A, I learn the atmosphere in London is:	Evidence from the text
• safe and secure	'can walk in most places after sunset'
• quiet, mysterious and lovely	'has a sedate and ghostly beauty'
•	
•	

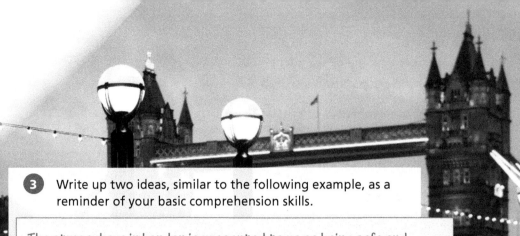

3 Write up two ideas, similar to the following example, as a reminder of your basic comprehension skills.

> The atmosphere in London is presented to us as being safe and secure and a place where you 'can walk in most places after sunset', which in some ways contradicts our perception of a modern day city after dark as it is often portrayed as dangerous.

Explore the skills

You are probably familiar with the technique for answering a comprehension question like the one in Activity 2 on a single text:

- *retrieve* key information
- *support* your idea with evidence
- demonstrate your understanding with an *inference*.

However, when showing your understanding of two texts, you need to be able to **synthesise** information quickly.

Read this second extract, from *Picturesque Sketches of London Past and Present*, by Thomas Miller, written in 1852.

Key term

synthesise: draw together information from one or more sources

Text B

There is something startling in the appearance of a vast city wrapt in a kind of darkness which seems neither to belong to the day nor the night, at the mid-noon hour, while the gas is burning in the windows of long miles of streets. The greatest marvel, after all, is that so few accidents happen in this dim, unnatural light, in the midst of which business seems to go on as usual, and would do, we believe, were the whole of London buried in midnight darkness at noonday, which would only be looked upon as a further deepening of the overhanging gloom. The number of lighted torches which are carried and waved at the corners and crossings of the streets add greatly to the wild and picturesque effect of the scene, as they flash redly upon the countenances of the passengers, and, in the distance, have the effect of a city enveloped in a dense mass of smoke, through which the smouldering flames endeavour in vain to penetrate.

During a heavy fog many accidents occur on the river, through barges running foul of each other, or vessels coming athwart the bridges; for there is no seeing the opening arch from the rock-like buttress, as the whole river looks like one huge bed of dense stagnant smoke, through which no human eye can penetrate. If you lean over the balustrades of the bridge, you cannot see the vessel which may at that moment be passing beneath, so heavy is the cloudy curtain which covers the water.

Thomas Miller, from *Picturesque Sketches of London Past and Present*

4 Look at this slightly different task from the ones in Activities 2 and 3.

> Summarise what you learn about the atmosphere of the city of London from the two texts.

What would you need to change or add to the method you used for Activity 3?

In order to write an effective summary of ideas, it is important to:

- ask yourself what the extracts have in common and what is different about them

- organise that information logically and clearly.

One effective way to gather your ideas is by using a Venn diagram like the one below to group the similarities and differences.

5 Copy and complete the diagram adding in any further ideas of your own.

London seems like a kind of fictional, fairytale place

Something mysterious and ghostly in both

London is a potentially dangerous place

London is a place where you can't tell day from night

The ideas in your Venn diagram will form the basis of your clear statements in completing the task.

Develop the skills

A further way to pull key ideas together is to consider quotations which link to the same topic or idea – even if they deal with it in a different way.

6 Look at the following quotations from Text A, then find a 'partner' quotation from Text B which deals with the same or a similar idea. The first one has been done as an example.

Text A

a 'It's a pretty safe city, and you can walk in most places after sunset.'

b 'It has a sedate and ghostly beauty'

c 'The river runs like dark silk through the heart of the city,'

d 'the bridges dance with light.'

e 'inky shadows'

f 'still illuminated by gaslight.'

Text B

'The greatest marvel, after all, is that so few accidents happen in this dim, unnatural light,'

7 For each pair of quotations you have collected, make notes on what is suggested by each pairing in relation to the atmosphere in London.

Now look at the example on the right of how a student has put together their statements, quotations and inferences on two texts in a clear and fluent way.

8 Write up a paragraph presenting one of your own ideas from Activity 5, supported by details or direct quotations from your pairing exercise in Activity 6 and including your inferences. Remember to use your quotations in one or more of the ways suggested in 3.2.

A.A. Gill asserts that the atmosphere in London has a 'sedate and ghostly beauty' about it, which makes the city seems like a romantic place, a place which is not quite real and suggests somewhere quiet, mysterious and lovely. Miller also presents London as having an atmosphere which seems supernatural in that the city is 'wrapt in a kind of darkness which seems neither to belong to the day nor the night'. This sounds less than romantic and suggests London in 1852 had a more menacing and threatening atmosphere than it does today.

Apply the skills

9 Using the techniques you have learned for comparing two texts, attempt the following task.

Summarise what you learn about the atmosphere of the city of London from the two texts.

Checklist for success

* Review the ideas from your Venn diagram and your quotation pairs.
* Write up four separate ideas.
* Use quotations in a sophisticated way.
* Make inferences to show your understanding and to complete the task.

Check your progress:

▲▲ I can present ideas from two texts in a detailed way, synthesising evidence from the texts and making perceptive inferences.

▲ I can present ideas from two texts in a fluent and clear way, with relevant quotations and/or close references and inference.

▲ I can present the ideas from two texts in a clear summary, supported by quotations and accompanied with inferences to show my understanding.

Apply your skills to English Language and English Literature tasks

Learning objectives
You will learn how to
• apply the key skills from this chapter to an unseen English Language task
• apply the key skills from this chapter to an English Literature task
• reflect on your progress through looking at different responses to both tasks.

Assessment objectives
• English Language AO1
• English Literature AO1

Responding to an English Language task

1 There are two texts below. One is from a broadsheet newspaper published recently; the other is an extract from a non-fiction text, 'The Crofter Question', from the early nineteenth century. As you read them, think about the following questions:

• What are these extracts about?

• What do we learn about the behaviour of people in authority today and in the past?

Text 1

Rio World Cup demolitions leave favela families trapped in ghost town

From the roof of his home in the Favela do Metrô, Eomar Freitas enjoys one of the best views in town. Look south and you see the Christ the Redeemer statue towering over Rio's mountains. To the north stands the green and pink headquarters of Mangueira, the city's best-loved samba school.

And in between, one of the world's top sporting venues, the blue and grey Maracanã stadium, which will host the final of the 2014 football World Cup.

'We worked hard to build this place,' said Freitas, 35 and unemployed, whose family moved to Rio from Brazil's impoverished north-east 20 years ago. They built a four-storey home where their wooden shack once stood. 'It was a great place to live,' he said.

Not any more. Since February, nearly all of the buildings surrounding Freitas's home have been levelled as part of work to revamp the city's infrastructure before the World Cup and the 2016 Olympic Games. Redbrick shacks have been cracked open by earth-diggers. Streets are covered in a thick carpet of rubble, litter and twisted metal. By night, crack addicts squat in abandoned shacks, filling sitting rooms with empty bottles, filthy mattresses and crack pipes improvised from plastic cups. The stench of human excrement hangs in the air.

'It looks like you are in Iraq or Libya,' Freitas said, wading across mounds of debris that now encircle his home. 'I don't have any neighbours left. It's a ghost town.'

[...]

Among them are elderly women and children, including a four-year-old boy with microcephaly and cerebral palsy.

'We ask God to support us, so our hearts don't give out,' said 77-year-old Sebastiana de Souza, who has spent 13 years in the favela, sharing a damp, cramped apartment with her daughter and four-year-old great-grandson who now plays football next to a heap of broken concrete, abandoned furniture and discarded toys. Souza said she hoped to be relocated to a nearby estate. 'It's sad. It used to be pretty around here.'

The reasons for the favela's demolition are disputed. Locals believe authorities plan to replace it with a car park for the nearby stadium, a story endorsed by one demolition worker.

'The World Cup is on its way and they want this area,' said Freitas. 'I think it is inhumane.'

Rio's housing secretary, Jorge Bittar, said the demolition was part of a £285m project to 'transform' the region around the Maracanã, itself the centre of a £330m pre-World Cup revamp. Cultural centres, tree-lined plazas and a cinema would be built, he said.

'This is a very poor community, with very precarious homes [built] in an inappropriate area and we are offering these families dignity,' he said.

Tom Phillips from *The Guardian*, 26 April 2011

Text 2

This extract comes from a report carried out into the forced removal
of families from the Scottish Highlands.

Mr. Ross went from Glasgow to Greenyard all the way to investigate the case upon the
spot, and found that Mr. Taylor, a native of Sutherland, well educated in the evicting
schemes and murderous cruelty of that county, and Sheriff-substitute of Ross-shire,
marched from Tain upon the morning of the 31st March, at the head of a strong party
of armed constables, with heavy bludgeons and firearms, conveyed in carts and other
vehicles, allowing them as much ardent drink as they chose to take before leaving and
on their march, so as to qualify them for the bloody work which they had to perform;
fit for any outrage, fully equipped, and told by the sheriff to show no mercy to anyone
who would oppose them, and not allow themselves to be called cowards, by allowing
these mountaineers victory over them. In this excited half-drunken state they came in
contact with the unfortunate women of Greenyard, who were determined to prevent
the officers from serving the summonses of removal upon them, and keep their holding
of small farms where they and their forefathers lived and died for generations. But
no time was allowed for parley; the sheriff gave the order to clear the way, and, be it
said to his everlasting disgrace, he struck the first blow at a woman, the mother of a
large family, and large in the family way at the time, who tried to keep him back; then
a general slaughter commenced; the women made noble resistance until the bravest
of them got their arms broken, then they gave way. This did not allay the rage of the
murderous brutes; they continued clubbing at the protectless creatures until every one
of them was stretched on the field, weltering in their blood, or with broken arms, ribs
and bruised limbs. In this woeful condition many of them were hand-cuffed together,
others tied with coarse ropes, huddled into carts, and carried prisoners to Tain.

Gilbert Beith, from 'The Crofter Question', 1884

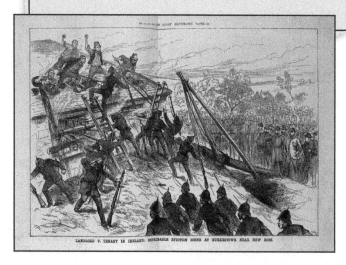

LANDLORD V. TENANT IN IRELAND: DEPLORABLE EVICTION SCENE AT BURKESTOWN, NEAR NEW ROSS.

2 Now read this practice task and consider how you would respond to it.

Your task

Using details from both sources, write a summary of the behaviour of the authorities towards the poor in Rio compared to in the Highlands in the past.

Checklist for success

Before you begin remember to:

- ask yourself which key ideas the extracts have in common and what ideas differ
- organise that information logically
- select evidence that you can use in support.

A successful response should include:

- clear statements in your own words addressing the question directly
- support for those statements with selected quotations
- inferences to show your understanding.

Reflecting on your progress

3 Read the following response to this task. As you read, think about what the student has done well and what advice they might need in order to make more progress.

Response 1

The broadsheet article tells us about how areas of Rio are being knocked down to 'revamp the city's infrastructure' before the World Cup of 2014, suggesting that the authorities feel they are doing something good for the area. In the past however, there is no suggestion that the removal of people is being done for everyone's benefit, as it describes the 'murderous cruelty' of the authorities.

makes a clear point about Text 1 with a supporting quotation

offers a direct contrast with Text 2, also with evidence

Lives are being destroyed in the favelas too as shown by the experience of Freitas who describes how he doesn't "'… have any neighbours left. It's a ghost town.'" There are also descriptions of how the place has been left in ruins, with 'a thick carpet of rubble, litter and twisted metal.' The destruction in the Highlands is very vicious as people are actually attacked and perhaps killed as the report describes how the sheriff's men 'continued clubbing at the protectless creatures until every one of them was stretched on the field, weltering in their blood…'

further new points made about the effects of the forced removal

The first article focuses on some of the positive things being done by the authorities, as claimed by Bittar, the housing secretary who says the homes in the favela are 'precarious' and in an 'inappropriate' place. By rebuilding around the Maracana the families will get 'dignity.' However, there is no dignity given to the people in the Highlands. The best example of this is that a pregnant woman who dares to stand up to the constables is 'struck' first.

clear contrasting point focused on the quote 'dignity'

develops comment on the 'dignity' issue

Another important thing is that there is no dignity in the way the people are removed. They are 'hand-cuffed together, others tied with coarse ropes, huddled into carts, and carried prisoners to Tain' which tells us that they were treated very inhumanely. It suggests there was no pretence about helping the crofters, they were simply seen as the enemy.

synthesises ideas but doesn't quite get to the heart of the differences

Comments on Response 1

This response focuses on the task and uses four separate ideas to build the summary. They find three clearly different ideas. Most ideas are supported with a useful and sensible quotation. There are inferences here – although some could be developed further and there is little synthesis of ideas.

4 How could this sample response be improved? Using the top rung of the Check your progress ladder at the end of this chapter, think about what advice you might give to this student in order to improve their work.

5 Now read Response 2. As you read, think about what the student has done that is an improvement on Response 1.

Response 2

While both texts deal with the behaviour of the authorities towards vulnerable people, there are clear differences in the extent and form of that behaviour. The first text deals with the longer term, more insidious effects of the so-called 'revamp', whilst the second describes the sudden and violent removal of residents in the 'evicting schemes.'

key point focuses on the immediacy of the removal

In the first text, we are given a clear indication of the after-effects of the programme of removal. The references to the 'thick carpet of rubble, litter and twisted metal' and Freitas's own comparison with Libya and Iraq suggest the aftermath of war, with the next battle soon to come. The idea of a battle is given even more prominence in Text 2 in the manner in which the Sheriff's men 'marched from Tain' and had 'armed constables, with heavy bludgeons and firearms.'

excellent point picks up on 'battle' references

The key difference is that the destruction is not done by diggers, but by drunken men who attack women. The fact that it is the Sheriff himself who, 'struck the first blow' implies his lack of shame, indeed even his appetite for the fight. In contrast, Rio's head of housing is keen to stress the 'dignity' he is giving to the people of the favelas, and the security, too, from their 'inappropriate' homes.

good point, supported by evidence and inferring further ideas

Both texts emphasise the idea that the authorities' behaviour impacts not just physically, but also emotionally on local people. In Text 1, Freitas says that 'We worked hard to build this place,' implying he had created something special and lasting for his family. Text 2 stresses this point even more strongly with the reference to the 'small farms where they and their forefathers lived and died for generations.' The constables are destroying not just the people and buildings, but their histories too.

new, distinct point of comparison

further point of difference which applies to the overall tone of the piece

Finally, by giving Freitas a voice in the first article, the effect of the authorities' rebuilding is personalised and, for all that has happened to him, he is able to express his opinions. In direct contrast, in Text 2, the women have no voice. The sheriff refuses to 'parley' and when they are 'hand-cuffed' and 'tied with coarse ropes, huddled into carts, and carried prisoners to Tain' they are treated no better than animals or slaves. The physical brutality removes all humanity from them.

excellent contrast with supporting evidence

Comments on Response 2

This excellent response picks up on a wide range of points of comparison and difference between the texts. It also develops each point, supports it with well-chosen evidence and explores the ramifications of it. The final paragraph focuses on a less obvious idea which is fluently explored and interpreted.

Responding to an English Literature task

1 Read the following extract from the opening to the short story, 'Odour of Chrysanthemums' by D.H. Lawrence. It is set around the beginning of the twentieth century when coal mining was still an important industry in the UK.

As you read, think about the following questions:

- What ideas is the writer **communicating** about the mother's world and her relationships?

- What do you notice about the ways language and structure have been used to communicate these ideas to the reader?

Miners, single, trailing and in groups, passed like shadows diverging home. At the edge of the ribbed level of sidings squat a low cottage, three steps down from the cinder track. A large bony vine clutched at the house, as if to claw down the tiled roof. Round the bricked yard grew a few wintry primroses. Beyond, the long garden sloped down to a bush-covered brook course. There were some twiggy apple trees, winter-crack trees, and ragged cabbages. Beside the path hung dishevelled pink chrysanthemums, like pink cloths hung on bushes. A woman came stooping out of the felt-covered fowl-house, half-way down the garden. She closed and padlocked the door, then drew herself erect, having brushed some bits from her white apron.
'Are you at that brook?' she asked sternly.
For answer the child showed himself before the raspberry-canes that rose like whips. He was a small, sturdy boy of five. He stood quite still, defiantly.
'Oh!' said the mother, conciliated. 'I thought you were down at that wet brook — and you remember what I told you —'
The boy did not move or answer.
'Come, come on in,' she said more gently, 'it's getting dark. There's your grandfather's engine coming down the line!'
The lad advanced slowly, with resentful, taciturn movement. He was dressed in trousers and waistcoat of cloth that was too thick and hard for the size of the garments. They were evidently cut down from a man's clothes.
As they went slowly towards the house he tore at the ragged wisps of chrysanthemums and dropped the petals in handfuls along the path.
'Don't do that — it does look nasty,' said his mother. He refrained, and she, suddenly pitiful, broke off a twig with three or four wan flowers and held them against her face. When mother and son reached the yard her hand hesitated, and instead of laying the flower aside, she pushed it in her apron-band.

D.H. Lawrence, from 'Odour of Chrysanthemums'

2 Now read this practice task and consider how you would respond to it.

Your task

'The opening to the story presents a bleak picture of the mother's world.'

How far do you agree with this statement?

Write about:

- the world created by Lawrence and his depiction of the relationship between the mother and her son

- how Lawrence presents these ideas.

Checklist for success

A successful response should:

- demonstrate your understanding of ideas in the story
- include some well-selected evidence
- make some inferences to demonstrate your understanding.

Reflecting on your progress

3 Read the following response to this task. As you read, think about what the student has done well and what advice they might need in order to make more progress.

Response 1

The extract begins with a detailed description of the mother's house and the surrounding area, which is close to the mine from the explanation of the miners who pass by 'single, trailing and in groups'. At this point, the writer is just providing a general description of the house and garden, but it is already clear that it is not going to be a happy tale. Words such as 'bony vine', 'claw' and 'wintry' are negative words and do not paint a pleasant picture. The paragraph ends with the woman being introduced.

The second paragraph gives a detailed picture of her. She is 'handsome' but it also tells us her 'mouth was closed with disillusionment.'
This suggests she has seen it all, there's nothing that surprises her. But at the moment we don't know why; is it her hard life or something else?

Then we find out she is worried about her son. In the first paragraph it mentioned a 'brook' at the end of the garden and when he doesn't answer we can guess she is worried he is playing near it. When he does reply it is with a 'sulky' voice which suggests their relationship is troubled – he doesn't want to tell her. In turn, she speaks 'sternly' which suggests she is going to tell him off and he replies 'defiantly' as if he is standing up to her.

As the extract continues he remains 'resentful' as if he objects to his mother's comments, and we begin to feel sympathy for him as his clothes are clearly much too big – 'they were evidently cut down from a man's clothes.' Then, his mother tells him off again for pulling off the flowers. We do begin to feel sorry for her though when she pulls off the 'wan flowers' and realise she is unhappy too.

Overall, they don't seem to have a very close relationship and this, added to the dark setting with the negative words used to describe the house and surroundings, makes a bitter image in our mind.

clear expression of textual style

carefully selected quotations

shows student is asking questions of him- or herself

draws inference about relationship

quotations embedded and brought together to make a point

understanding shown of mother's role but missing what we might infer about her attitude to son

Comments on Response 1

This response shows a clear understanding of the text in terms of the mother and her son, and also makes some comment on the 'world' Lawrence creates. The student also draws some basic inferences about the mother's relationship with the son, and the quotations from which inferences are drawn are generally well-chosen. Expression is clear throughout.

4 How could this sample response be improved? Using the top rung of the Check your progress ladder at the end of this chapter, think about what advice you might give to this student in order to improve their work.

5 Now read Response 2. As you read, think about what the student has done that is an improvement on Response 1.

Response 2

From the opening description of the miners who pass 'like shadows', a sense of gloom pervades the text. The miners are aimless in how they walk, and this sense of passivity is developed throughout the extract. Even the 'bony vine', personified in the way it clasps the house, restricts movement, as if choking the building. Everything seems to be decaying or wilting – the adjectives such as 'twiggy apple-trees', 'ragged cabbages', and 'dishevelled ... chrysanthemums' all suggest a world which is dead or dying.

When the writer introduces the mother, at least her strength comes through as she is 'imperious' and watches 'steadily'. These are positive images but it is not all rosy as her 'mouth was closed with disillusionment'. She understands the world and if she once had any innocence she doesn't any more, although why is not clear at this point.

Her relationship with her son may be the reason, although there is a strange mix of care and conflict between them. She speaks 'sternly' to him, but this is because she is worried he has being playing at the stream. When he replies he stands 'defiantly' which suggests two strong wills battling against each other.

clear understanding of the importance of opening sentence in creating Lawrence's world

excellent critical style which draws ideas together

apt quotations fluently embedded into response showing real insight

sustained focus on the relationship created by Lawrence

But when she tells him to come in she speaks 'gently', although this does not soften the boy's mood as he moves in a 'resentful' way. The reader then sees that he is dressed very poorly, wearing adult clothes cut down to fit him, and this perhaps gives one ——— reason for the mother's 'disillusionment'. It is like she is trying to keep up the appearance of being someone respectable, but reality keeps breaking in.

begins to answer question raised earlier

This last idea is further emphasised when the boy tears at the ——— flowers in a violent way, and lets them drop on the path, like litter. He gets told off, again, but our sympathies are, in fact, directed to the mother as she smells the 'wan flowers' which she pulls off, as if trying to inject something beautiful into the dying world.

further development of ideas, inferred from key moment in text

Overall, the extract presents a picture of a problematic ——— relationship between mother and child, but this is overcome by the empathy we feel for this proud woman trying to retain something of beauty in her drab existence.

excellent overview of mother and her place in this setting

Comments on Response 2

This demonstrates in-depth understanding and insight, and fluently embeds evidence and quotation. The critical style and vocabulary is varied yet sustained and enables the student to make links between ideas. There is both detailed comment and a wider overview of the 'world' and relationships.

Check your progress

- I can read and understand more challenging texts, selecting information and showing a perceptive understanding.

- I can select and use a range of quotations and/or close textual references in a sophisticated way.

- I can present ideas from two texts in a detailed way, synthesising evidence from the texts and making perceptive inferences.

- I can read more challenging texts, selecting information and clearly showing my understanding.

- I can select and use relevant quotations and/or close textual references.

- I can present ideas from two texts in a fluent and clear way, with relevant quotations and/or close references and inference.

- I can read unfamiliar texts, selecting information and clearly showing my understanding.

- I can choose quotations carefully to support my points.

- I can present the ideas from two texts in a clear summary, supported by quotations and accompanied with inferences to show my understanding.

Chapter 4

Analysing and evaluating writers' methods and effects

What's it all about?

In this chapter, you will learn how to analyse and evaluate the conscious decisions writers make about the ways they manipulate language, structure and form in order to create meanings and effects. You will learn how to establish a writer's overall viewpoint and then select precise details of the ways they communicate these ideas to their readers, considering these very closely and linking them to the overall meanings being communicated.

In this chapter, you will learn how to

- analyse and evaluate writers' use of language techniques
- analyse and evaluate writers' use of structure
- analyse the ways writers create meanings and effects with structure and form
- apply your skills to English Language and English Literature tasks.

	English Language GCSE	English Literature GCSE
Which AOs are covered?	AO2 Explain, comment on and analyse how writers use language and structure to achieve effects and influence readers, using linguistic terminology to support their views	AO2 Analyse the language and methods used by a writer to achieve specific purposes and effects, using relevant subject terminology where appropriate
How will this be tested?	Some questions will ask you to focus in detail on particular words and phrases. Others will identify a particular area of a text and ask you to look closely at the meanings and techniques being used in that particular part. All the texts you will be responding to will be previously unseen.	Wider questions will ask you to analyse and comment on the overall text, paying attention to the language, the structure or the literary techniques being used by the writer to communicate meanings and create effects. Sometimes you will be responding to a whole play or novel that you have studied in class and sometimes you will be writing about two previously unseen poems.

Analyse and evaluate writers' use of language techniques

Learning objectives
You will learn how to
- analyse the ways writers use particular techniques in order to communicate meanings to their readers
- make precise selections of particular techniques to analyse in detail.

Assessment objective
- English Language AO2

What does 'analyse the effect' mean and how do you do it successfully?

Getting you thinking

Analysing the effects of writers' language techniques means you are focused on the craft of the writer and the range of ways they are using language to communicate ideas to their readers. Knowing and using the correct terms for writers' techniques provides you with a useful shorthand for analysing what they are doing more effectively.

In this section of *The Road to Wigan Pier*, George Orwell uses a range of language techniques in order to express a particular viewpoint.

A slag-heap is at best a hideous thing, because it is so planless and functionless. It is something just dumped on the earth, like the emptying of a giant's dust-bin. ⟶ **simile** On the outskirts of the mining towns there are frightful landscapes where your horizon is ringed completely round by jagged grey mountains, and underfoot is mud and ashes and overhead the steel cables where tubs of dirt travel slowly across miles of country. Often the slag-heaps are on fire, ⟶ **alliteration** and at night you can see the red rivulets of fire winding this way and that, and also the slow-moving blue flames of sulphur, which always seem on the point of expiring and always spring out again. Even when a slag-heap sinks, as it does ultimately, only an evil brown grass grows on it, ⟶ **personification** and it retains its hummocky surface. One in the slums of Wigan, used as a playground, looks ⟶ **simile** like a choppy sea suddenly frozen; 'the flock mattress', it is called locally. Even centuries hence when the plough drives over the places where coal was once mined, the sites of ancient slag-heaps will still be distinguishable from an aeroplane.

George Orwell, from *The Road to Wigan Pier*

1. Choose one of the techniques and write a short paragraph in your own words explaining why you think Orwell has used it, and what effect you think it creates. Think about:
   - the mood or atmosphere being created
   - how particular words / phrases make you feel
   - the image created by particular words / phrases.

Key terms

simile: form of comparison using 'as' or 'like'

alliteration: repetition of a sound, usually (but not always) at the start of a sequence of words

personification: a type of metaphor where an inanimate object is given human characteristics such as emotions

Explore the skills

Look at the following example of a student's response to this activity.

> Orwell uses the simile 'like a giant's dust-bin' to suggest that the slag-heap is enormous and disgusting. It makes the reader imagine a huge heap of rubbish, and creates a kind of monstrous feeling to the picture with the use of the word 'giant'. It suggests that this amount of waste is out of human control.

identifies the correct technique and uses the right terminology

evidence is embedded fluently into the student's sentence

focuses in detail on particular words in the phrase they have chosen

starts to explore the **connotations** of particular effects of the simile

2 Now read the next section of the text. Find one example of each technique:

- simile
- metaphor
- personification.

> At night, when you cannot see the hideous shapes of the houses and the blackness of everything, a town like Sheffield assumes a kind of sinister magnificence. Sometimes the drifts of smoke are rosy with sulphur, and serrated flames, like circular saws, squeeze themselves out from beneath the cowls of the foundry chimneys. Through the open doors of foundries you see fiery serpents of iron being hauled to and fro by redlit boys, and you hear the whizz and thump of steam hammers and the scream of the iron under the blow.

Key term

connotations: ideas, feelings, associations and connections between words and ideas that are additional to the literal meaning

Take a closer look at the metaphor: 'fiery serpents of iron'.
What connotations can be drawn from this metaphor?

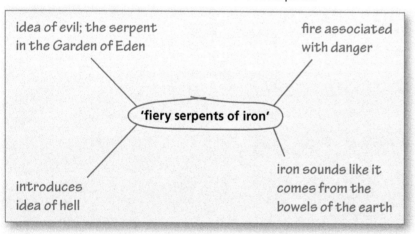

idea of evil; the serpent
in the Garden of Eden

fire associated
with danger

'fiery serpents of iron'

introduces
idea of hell

iron sounds like it
comes from the
bowels of the earth

3 Write a paragraph in your own words about the effects of
this metaphor, using some of the ideas in the spider diagram
above to help you.

Develop the skills

One of the techniques Orwell uses in this passage is a **semantic field**
of danger.

4 Read the passage again and make a list of all the words and
phrases he uses that have connotations of danger.

Key term

semantic field: a group or
collection of words that have
a similar meaning or create
similar ideas in the mind of the
reader

5 Read the passage again and answer the following questions.

    a What is Orwell suggesting about how it must feel to live and work there through his use of this semantic field?

    b Orwell is using a semantic field here to create an **extended metaphor**. What is he comparing the place to, and what does this suggest about his view of the place?

Orwell is also using personification again to add to the extended metaphor with the phrase 'scream of the iron under the blow'.

Key term

extended metaphor: a metaphor developed over a sequence of text

6 Discuss with a partner what you think the effect of this image might be. How does it link to some of the other techniques you have identified in this passage?

Analysing specific language techniques and relating them to the overall viewpoint is a high-level skill. Use the two questions below to develop a paragraph of no more than 100 words, relating one or two techniques to Orwell's overall viewpoint.

7 **a** How does Orwell use language techniques to intensify the image of danger in the mind of the reader?

    b How does the use of particular techniques help to communicate Orwell's viewpoint about living in this part of the country?

Apply the skills

8 Now you have read the extracts and identified some of the ways language techniques are being used, you are ready to form a response to a question.

How does Orwell use language techniques to suggest that the industrial north of England is a dangerous, unhealthy place to live?

Select two or three specific features in order to create a more developed response. You don't have to write about everything. Link your analysis to Orwell's overall viewpoint and purpose.

Checklist for success

- What is Orwell suggesting about life for the people who live in the industrial north of England?
- Explore Orwell's use of imagery (similes, metaphors, personification).
- How does Orwell use extended metaphors and semantic fields?

Check your progress:

- I can present a succinct overview of the writer's viewpoint and select one or more language techniques to analyse this viewpoint thoroughly and in detail.

- I can select and analyse particular language techniques in detail, linking them precisely to the writer's viewpoint.

- I can choose clear supporting evidence to explain how one or more language techniques help to communicate the writer's viewpoint.

Analyse and evaluate writers' use of structure

Learning objective
You will learn how to
- analyse some of the ways writers use structure and organisational features in non-fiction texts in order to express a particular viewpoint.

Assessment objective
- English Language AO2

How do structure and organisation make a difference to the ways in which a text is read and understood?

Getting you thinking

Imagine this scenario.

> You are a journalist. You have been commissioned to write a 500-word **op-ed article** called 'Women and Weight' for a national broadsheet lifestyle magazine. If your article is accepted, you will receive a substantial payment, and your work may be read by thousands of people.

What do you think of this as a starting point?

> I think that there is a real problem with women and weight in this country at the moment. Women are getting fatter all the time, and this is causing real health problems for the country. Forty years ago the average size was a size 10, and now it is a 16. Women are made to feel bad about this, and because of this they often hide their problem and become secret eaters, which only makes the problem worse.

Key term

op-ed article: an article or essay in a newspaper, expressing the opinions or viewpoint of a writer who does not work for that newspaper

1 Does this opening grab your attention?

2 Now read the first paragraph from 'How to be a Woman' by Caitlin Moran on the same subject.

> Why did I get fat? Why was I eating until I hurt and regarding my own body as something as distant and unsympathetic as, say, the state of the housing market in Buenos Aires? Obviously, it's not wholly advisable to swell up so large that, on one very bad day, you get stuck in a bucket seat at a local fair and have to be rescued by your old schoolmaster, but why is being fat treated as a cross between terrible shame and utter tragedy? Something that – for a woman – is seen as falling somewhere between sustaining a sizable facial scar and sleeping with the Nazis?
>
> Caitlin Moran, from *How to be a Woman*

3 What is your response to this opening paragraph?

    a Is it better than the first one? If so, why?

    b What is Moran's viewpoint on being overweight?

    c What kind of tone is being created in this introduction?

Explore the skills

4 Look at this list of some of the structural techniques Moran uses in her first paragraph. Identify an example of each:

- very short sentence
- **rhetorical question**
- **hyperbolic question**
- personal **anecdote**
- dashes to emphasise a particular idea (or ideas).

This is how one student commented on Moran's use of dashes.

> *The dashes do the same job as brackets but are more informal, which fits with the overall tone. However, Moran seems to be suggesting that the issue of being overweight is seen as much more important 'for a woman' by separating this phrase with the dashes. She might be implying it is wrong that women in particular, rather than men, are made to feel bad about their weight.*

Key terms

rhetorical question: a question which is designed to make the reader think, not to answer directly

hyperbolic question: an exaggerated question designed to make a particular point

anecdote: a short personal story designed to add humour or illustrate a point

5 Choose another one of the techniques and write a short paragraph explaining how you think the technique helps to emphasise Moran's viewpoint.

Moran uses personal anecdotes deliberately. In the article, the anecdote sounds as if it is just an example. Do you think it might have actually happened? If so, why does she not say this directly?

Read the next paragraph of Moran's article. As you read, notice how she uses parentheses (brackets).

> Why will women happily boast-moan about spending too much ('…and then my bank manager took my credit card and cut it in half with a sword!'), about drinking too much ('…and then I took my shoe off and threw it over the bus stop!'), and about working too hard ('…so tired I fell asleep on the control panel, and when I woke up, I realized I'd pressed the nuclear launch button! Again!') but never, ever about eating too much? Why is unhappy eating the most pointlessly secret of miseries? It's not like you can hide a six-Kit-Kats-a-day habit for very long.

6 What have the sections in parentheses got in common? What kind of tone do they help to create?

7 How many rhetorical questions has Moran used in the first two paragraphs? What is the purpose of all the questions and how do they help to communicate her viewpoint to the reader?

Develop the skills

Now read the final three paragraphs of the article.

I sometimes wonder if the only way we'll ever get around to properly considering overeating is if it does come to take on the same perverse, rock 'n' roll cool of other addictions. Perhaps it's time for women to finally stop being secretive about their vices and instead start treating them like all other addicts treat their habits. Coming into the office looking frazzled, sighing, 'Man, I was on the pot roast last night like you wouldn't believe. I had, like, MASH in my EYEBROWS by 10 p.m.'

Then people would be able to address your dysfunction as openly as they do all the others. They could reply, 'Whoa, maybe you should calm it down for a bit, my friend. I am the same. I did a three-hour session on the microwave lasagna last night. Perhaps we should go out to the country for a bit. Clean up our acts.'

Because at the moment, I can't help but notice that in a society obsessed with fat – so eager in the appellation, so vocal in its disapproval – the only people who aren't talking about it are the only people whose business it really is.

8 What is the difference between the tone at the start and at the end of the article? Which one is the more serious? Why do you think Moran has structured her text in this way?

Always establish the overall point the writer is making. If you are clear about this, you can link your comments on the writer's effects much more clearly to the purpose of the writing.

9 What is Moran's overall viewpoint in this article? Consider the following statements and decide which you think are the most appropriate.

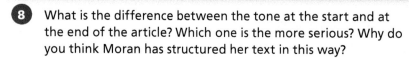

Moran thinks that weight is a real issue in this society.

Moran thinks that attitudes towards weight are a real issue in this society.

Moran thinks that women are ashamed of their weight and the stigma surrounding it in this society.

Moran thinks that weight shouldn't be taken seriously.

Apply the skills

10 Look at the following short quotation from Moran's book and the student notes about it.

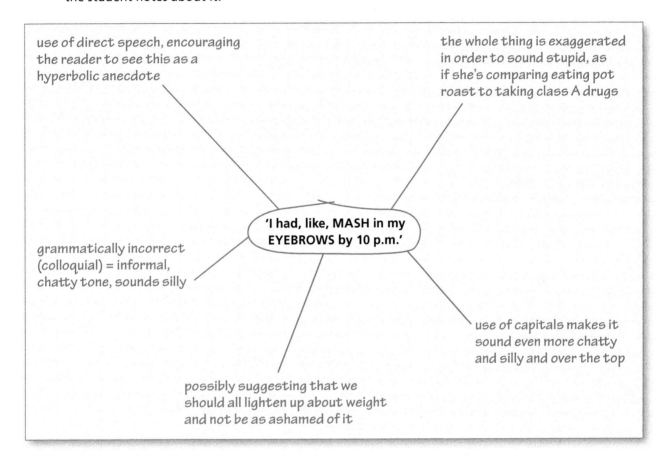

use of direct speech, encouraging the reader to see this as a hyperbolic anecdote

the whole thing is exaggerated in order to sound stupid, as if she's comparing eating pot roast to taking class A drugs

'I had, like, MASH in my EYEBROWS by 10 p.m.'

grammatically incorrect (colloquial) = informal, chatty tone, sounds silly

use of capitals makes it sound even more chatty and silly and over the top

possibly suggesting that we should all lighten up about weight and not be as ashamed of it

11 Choose a different section of the text and annotate it in the same way. When you have finished your annotations, complete the following task.

> Write an analysis of the ways Moran uses structure and organisation to present her ideas. Aim to write 250–300 words.

Checklist for success
....
- Focus on the ways in which Moran has structured and organised her ideas.
- How has she used this structure to communicate her viewpoint to the reader?

Check your progress:
....

- I can analyse the effects of particular structural features in detail, exploring how they have been used to present the writer's viewpoint.

- I can consider a range of ways in which a writer has used structural features to present their viewpoint.

- I can clearly explain the ways one or more structural features have been used to present a viewpoint.

Analyse the ways writers create meanings and effects with structure and form

Learning objective
You will learn how to
- analyse some of the ways that writers use structure and form to create meanings in poetry.

Assessment objective
- English Literature AO2

What is the difference between 'structure' and 'form'?
Why does the 'form' of a text matter?

> **Getting you thinking**

Sometimes the differences between 'structure' and 'form' can be a little difficult to unpick and thoroughly understand. This is because they overlap.

'Structure' refers to any device or mechanism used to order and create overall cohesion in a text.

'Form' refers to a prescribed set of organisational rules for a particular type of text.

This can be confusing because when you are looking at form, you are looking at the way a text has been structured!

1 **a** Look at the following question and the possible answers below. Decide which are true.

What is a sonnet?

• a form of poetry	• is usually about love
• has fourteen lines	• has a defined rhyme scheme
• is written in iambic pentameter	• can be divided into four stanzas or two stanzas
• ends with a rhyming couplet	

b Which of the statements refer to structure? Which one of the statements is only partially, or sometimes, true?

Explore the skills

Look at the following poem. It was written in the sixteenth century.

> **Sonnet 75**
>
> One day I wrote her name upon the strand,
> But came the waves and washèd it away:
> Again I wrote it with a second hand,
> But came the tide, and made my pains his prey.
>
> 'Vain man,' said she, 'that dost in vain assay,
> A mortal thing so to immortalize,
> For I myself shall like to this decay,
> And eek my name be wipèd out likewise.'
>
> 'Not so,' quod I, 'let baser things devise
> To die in dust, but you shall live by fame:
> My verse your virtues rare shall eternise,
> And in the heavens write your glorious name.
>
> Where when as death shall all the world subdue,
> Our love shall live, and later life renew.'
>
> Edmund Spenser

This is written using the Shakespearean sonnet form. It has four stanzas: three stanzas of four lines and one final rhyming couplet. There is a strict rhyme scheme of ABAB, CDCD, EFEF, GG.

The ideas in the poem are common to lots of sonnets. On the surface, sonnets are often about love, but will also deal with other 'big', universal ideas about the human condition.

2 Reread the poem, exploring the following questions.

a What is each stanza 'about' – what is the content of each one?

b What is the overall poem 'about' – what is the main idea being explored?

c Is this poem just about love, or is Spenser also exploring something else?

Develop the skills

A Petrarchan sonnet is made up of two stanzas: an octave (eight lines) and a sestet (six lines). There is a **volta** between the octave and the sestet. Often the octave sets up a question or dilemma, which is resolved in the sestet. The sestet will have a different rhyme scheme to the octave, marking the change in direction.

The following poem, 'How to Leave the World that Worships *Should*' by Ros Barber, is in the form of a Petrachan sonnet, but was written only recently.

Key term

volta: change of direction in a sonnet, used to mark a turn in thought

3 As you read, make notes in response to the following questions.

a What do you think this poem is about? Is it about love or something else?

b What changes between the octet and the sestet? What is different about the meaning between the two stanzas?

Key terms

enjambment: continuing a sentence or clause over a line break to delay closure and increase anticipation

caesura: a break or pause in the flow of a line, often used to emphasise key ideas, words or moments

---

How to Leave the World that Worships *Should*

Let **faxes** butter-curl on dusty shelves.
Let junkmail build its castles in the hush
of other people's halls. Let deadlines burst ——————— enjambment
and flash like glorious fireworks somewhere else.
As hours go softly by, let others curse ——————— caesura
the roads where distant drivers queue like sheep.
Let e-mails fly like panicked, tiny birds.
Let phones, unanswered, ring themselves to sleep.

Above, the sky unrolls its telegram,
immense and wordless, simply understood:
you've made your mark like birdtracks in the sand —
now make the air in your lungs your livelihood.
See how each wave arrives at last to heave
itself upon the beach and vanish. Breathe.

Ros Barber

Glossary

faxes: an early form of technical communication in the 1980s

Apply the skills

Now you are more familiar with the structural conventions, or rules, of the sonnet form, you are in a stronger position to start to analyse how the writer might have adapted particular features of the form to create particular effects.

 Complete the following task, using the prompts below to help you.

> How does Ros Barber use structure and form to explore her ideas about life in 'How to Leave the World that Worships *Should*'?

Aim to write around 300 words and to use correct technical vocabulary where appropriate. Use the following prompts to support your analysis.

• All the lines in 'How to Leave the World that Worships *Should*' conform to the rhythm of the sonnet form apart from one:

> *now make the air in your lungs your livelihood.*

Why might Barber have given this line more syllables than all the others? What effect might she be trying to create by adapting the form in this way?

• The final line of the poem contains a sentence of just one word. Why might Barber have decided to structure the final line of the poem in this way? What effect might she be trying to create?

• How does Barber use other structural features, such as caesura and enjambment, to present her ideas?

• If this poem isn't about romantic love, why do you think Barber has used a sonnet form to present her ideas? Is there any other kind of love in the poem?

Checklist for success

• Consider how the poem conforms to the rhythm of the sonnet.

• Look at how structural features, such as caesura and enjambment, are used to present ideas.

• Consider why the sonnet form is used to present the poet's ideas.

Check your progress:

 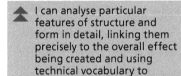

I can analyse significant features of form and structure, linking them together to explore how a writer has manipulated them in order to create particular meanings.

I can analyse particular features of structure and form in detail, linking them precisely to the overall effect being created and using technical vocabulary to explain effects.

I can explain some features of structure or form, making links to the effects being created and making accurate use of technical vocabulary.

Apply your skills to English Language and English Literature tasks

Learning objectives
You will learn how to
* apply the key skills from this chapter to two unseen English Language tasks
* apply the key skills from this chapter to one English Literature text
* reflect on your progress through looking at some exemplar responses to both tasks.

Assessment objectives
* English Language AO2
* English Literature AO2

Responding to an English Language task: Language

The following extract is from the first chapter of the novel *Lord of the Flies*.

 As you read it, think about and make some immediate notes on the following questions:

a What is this extract about?

b What are we learning about the boys and about where they are?

c How has the writer used language and structure to communicate ideas to the reader?

The Sound of the Shell

The boy with fair hair lowered himself down the last few feet of rock and began to pick his way toward the lagoon. Though he had taken off his school sweater and trailed it now from one hand, his grey shirt stuck to him and his hair was plastered to his forehead. All round him the long scar smashed into the jungle was a bath of heat. He was clambering heavily among the creepers and broken trunks when a bird, a vision of red and yellow, flashed upwards with a witch-like cry; and this cry was echoed by another.

'Hi!' it said. 'Wait a minute!'

The undergrowth at the side of the scar was shaken and a multitude of raindrops fell pattering.

'Wait a minute,' the voice said. 'I got caught up.'

The fair boy stopped and jerked his stockings with an automatic gesture that made the jungle seem for a moment like the Home Counties.

The voice spoke again.

'I can't hardly move with all these creeper things.'

The owner of the voice came backing out of the undergrowth so that twigs scratched on a greasy wind-breaker. The naked crooks of his knees were plump, caught and scratched by thorns. He bent down, removed the thorns carefully, and turned around. He was shorter than the fair boy and very fat. He came forward, searching out safe lodgments for his feet, and then looked up through thick spectacles.

'Where's the man with the megaphone?'

The fair boy shook his head.

'This is an island. At least I think it's an island. That's a reef out in the sea. Perhaps there aren't any grownups anywhere.'

The fat boy looked startled.

'There was that pilot. But he wasn't in the passenger cabin, he was up in front.'

The fair boy was peering at the reef through screwed-up eyes.

'All them other kids,' the fat boy went on. 'Some of them must have got out. They must have, mustn't they?'

The fair boy began to pick his way as casually as possible toward the water. He tried to be offhand and not too obviously uninterested, but the fat boy hurried after him.

'Aren't there any grownups at all?'

'I don't think so.'

William Golding, from *Lord of the Flies*

2   Now look at this practice task and consider how you would respond to it.

Your task

Look in detail at this part of the extract.

> The boy with fair hair lowered himself down the last few feet of rock and began to pick his way toward the lagoon. Though he had taken off his school sweater and trailed it now from one hand, his grey shirt stuck to him and his hair was plastered to his forehead. All round him the long scar smashed into the jungle was a bath of heat. He was clambering heavily among the creepers and broken trunks when a bird, a vision of red and yellow, flashed upwards with a witch-like cry; and this cry was echoed by another.
>
> 'Hi!' it said. 'Wait a minute!'
>
> The undergrowth at the side of the scar was shaken and a multitude of raindrops fell pattering.
>
> 'Wait a minute,' the voice said. 'I got caught up.'
>
> The fair boy stopped and jerked his stockings with an automatic gesture that made the jungle seem for a moment like the Home Counties.
>
> The voice spoke again.
>
> 'I can't hardly move with all these creeper things.'

How does the writer's use of language here create an impression that the boys are lost in an unfamiliar place?

Checklist for success

A successful response should include:

- reference to particular words and phrases
- comments on the effects of language features and techniques
- comments on the effects of sentence forms and punctuation.

Reflecting on your progress

3   Read the following response to this task. As you read, think about what the student has done well and what advice they might need in order to make more progress.

Response 1

The writer makes the place seem unfamiliar to the boy straight away. It says that the boy 'lowered himself' and 'began to pick his way'. This suggests that he doesn't know the place so is moving carefully and slowly, as if he is cautious. The writer then mentions his 'school sweater', which creates the impression that the boy is out of place here as there is a 'lagoon' and they are in a 'jungle', which makes his school jumper out of place.

The boy seems uncomfortable and not used to the heat. He is described as 'clambering heavily' and he is obviously suffering from the heat of the jungle. The adverb 'heavily' suggests this is hard for him. The writer also uses adjectives, such as describing him having a 'grey shirt' which is 'stuck to him', again sounding like a school uniform that is out of place. When he hears the other voice he pulls his school socks up, which makes it sound like he is used to rules and gets into trouble for not wearing his uniform properly. Again this seems out of place and like he is used to school life, not being in the jungle. When the boy hears a bird he doesn't mention what kind of bird it is, as though it isn't something he is familiar with. When the second boy comes in he refers to the jungle growth as 'creeper things' which again sounds as if this is unfamiliar territory for the boys; they don't know what the creepers are, and are not used to moving around and through them.

The writer also talks about a 'scar smashed into the jungle' which is probably from some kind of accident. The word 'scar' suggests pain and danger as if the boy is in a dangerous situation here.

Annotations:
- effective use of embedded evidence
- clear inferences about the effect of particular language choices
- good use of detail here, linked to some good inferences
- correct use of subject terminology
- more useful embedded evidence to support idea about boy being out of place
- good comment – meanings rather than language?
- much better comment on language here
- good comment on language effects

Comments on Response 1

This is a clear and developed response with some very effective use of evidence. There are several points about the effect of particular word choices which indicate a very good understanding of the passage and the ways language has been used. However, there is a tendency to stray into ideas / inferences once or twice, rather than focusing precisely on the language.

4 How could this sample response be improved? Using the middle rung of the Check your progress ladder at the end of this chapter, think about what advice you might give to this student in order to improve their work.

5 Now read Response 2. As you read, think about what the student has done that is an improvement on Response 1, and what advice this student might need in order to make even more progress.

Response 2

> The jungle atmosphere is created through the references to a 'bath of heat' and the first boy's evident discomfort with it: it 'stuck to him', was 'plastered to his forehead'. This sense of the boy being in unfamiliar territory is reinforced by the contrast between the descriptive language used to describe the place and the description of the boy: 'lagoon' / 'jungle' / 'creepers' are in stark contrast to the boy's 'school jumper' / 'grey shirt' / 'stockings'. This creates the sense that the boys are out of place and in alien territory outside the safe and ordered environment of school. The sense of unfamiliarity and danger is created by the violent imagery of 'smashed', 'flashed' and 'scar'. The mention of the nameless 'bird' not only reinforces the sense that the boy is in an unfamiliar place as he can't name it, but also hints at a tropical location with the adjectives 'red and yellow'. These colours also add to the sense of heat and danger with the connotations of fire they suggest.

— lovely contrast between language effects

— focused comment on language effects

— analysis of description of bird

Comments on Response 2

This response is much more focused on the effects of language choices. The analysis of the description of the bird is particularly skilful as it looks at a range of ways this detail creates particular effects.

Responding to an English Language task: Structure

1 Now look at this practice task and consider how you would respond to it.

Your task

You now need to think about the whole extract from *Lord of the Flies* and the ways in which Golding has structured his writing.

This extract is from the opening to a novel. How has the writer used structure within the extract to interest the reader?

Checklist for success

A successful response should include:

* what the writer focuses your attention on at the very start
* what else the writer draws your attention to as the extract develops
* any other structural features that interest you as a reader.

Reflecting on your progress

2 Read the following response to this task. As you read, think about what the student has done well and what advice they might need in order to make more progress.

Response 1

The first paragraph of the story focuses the reader's attention on the place, and the contrast between the place and the boys. The place is clearly some kind of tropical island with 'lagoon' and 'creepers' and 'jungle'. The boy is out of place here – he is wearing school uniform, he is uncomfortably hot and he doesn't know the names of things, such as the nameless 'bird' that startles him. The writer is making it clear from the start that the boys are lost.

This idea is developed, as the extract goes on. The second boy is clearly just as lost and out of place, he 'backs out' of the undergrowth, showing that he is very uncomfortable and can't move around properly. It makes him sound awkward and out of place. This is reinforced with the way his knees are described as 'naked' and 'scratched', as if he is vulnerable. The dialogue between the boys is lots of short, simple sentences. This suggests they are perhaps tense.

The extract ends with the news that the boys are on their own. They realise that there are no 'grown ups' there. This is a shocking way to draw the reader in, as for the children to be on their own in such an unfamiliar place would be very frightening and would certainly make the reader want to find out what will happen to them.

good focus on the effect of the start of the extract and what the writer is drawing attention to

moving on to the ways the extract develops

focusing in more on how the writer is showing important details about the boys

focus on the type of sentences being used and the effects they create

clear development through the extract

good comment on the effect of the ending of the extract

Comments on Response 1

This response focuses clearly on the task, with good focus on the start, middle and end of the extract. Comments are supported well with relevant, useful quotation throughout, and there is evidence that the student has a sound grasp of the ideas and the writer's purpose. There is some mention of sentence types, but this is rather brief and could be much more developed.

3 How could this sample response be improved? Using the middle rung of the Check your progress ladder at the end of this chapter, think about what advice you might give to this student in order to improve their work.

4 Now read Response 2. As you read, think about what the student has done that is an improvement on Response 1, and what advice this student might need in order to make even more progress.

Response 2

> The writer uses the first few lines to foreground the place — it is the place that is clearly going to be very significant. The first paragraph contrasts the boy with the unfamiliar jungle, emphasising how out of place and alone he is with his 'school jumper' and 'grey shirt', as if he is a school boy in an alien world. The ambiguous 'scar smashed into the jungle' creates an immediate sense of violence and threat, as it is presumably from some kind of air accident. However, the writer doesn't explain this, leaving the reader to find out gradually what has happened. The entrance of the second boy emphasises and builds on this idea. This boy is even less comfortable and more out of place than the first one, and he is shown to be frightened and vulnerable. The writer develops this sense of the boys being abandoned and isolated, looking for the names of the unfamiliar 'things' they see around them. The second boy talks about the 'pilot', which links back to the first paragraph and hints that there has been a crash. The final lines create a sense of shock and isolation with the shortness of the blunt statement; 'I don't think so'. The writer is taking the reader on a journey, we are discovering the island in the same way that the boys are, looking at it one detail at a time.

- strong overview of the purpose of the opening lines
- focus on effect of structural elements on reader
- building the response here
- development of an idea begun earlier, showing grasp of the structural effects of the extract as a whole
- insightful comment on the effect of perspective and structure

Comments on Response 2

This response takes more of an overview of the writer's purpose, looking at the structure of the extract as a whole and the effects of the way it starts and gradually builds. This is a confident, purposeful response to the task with a strong sense of the writer's use of structure and its effect on the reader.

Responding to an English Literature task

1. Read the following poem, 'The Swan' by Mary Oliver. As you read, think about the following questions:
   - What is this poem about?
   - What ideas and feelings do you think the writer is communicating?
   - What do you notice about the ways language and structure have been used to communicate these ideas and feelings to the reader?

The Swan

Did you too see it, drifting, all night, on the black river?

Did you see it in the morning, rising into the silvery air –
An armful of white blossoms,

A perfect commotion of silk and linen as it leaned into
the bondage of its wings; a snowbank, a bank of lilies,

Biting the air with its black beak?

Did you hear it, fluting and whistling

A shrill dark music – like the rain pelting the trees –
like a waterfall

Knifing down the black ledges?

And did you see it, finally, just under the clouds –
A white cross streaming across the sky, its feet

Like black leaves, its wings

Like the stretching light of the river?

And did you feel it, in your heart, how it pertained
to everything?

And have you too finally figured out what beauty is for?

And have you changed your life?

Mary Oliver

2 Now look at this practice task and consider how you would
respond to it.

Your task
How does the writer use the image of the swan to explore ideas
about life in this poem?

Checklist for success
A successful response should:

- demonstrate your understanding of the writer's ideas and
  feelings

- include some well-selected evidence

- analyse the effects of particular words, literary techniques
  and structural features, linked to the ideas and feelings in the
  poem.

Reflecting on your progress

3   Read the following response to this task. As you read, think about what the student has done well and what advice they might need in order to make more progress.

Response 1

> The poet uses imagery of black and white throughout the poem. This creates contrast and links to an idea of opposite forces. The river is 'black' but the bird rises into 'silvery' air, described like 'an armful of white blossoms'. The bird is also compared to 'snowbank' and 'lilies', which reinforces the image of whiteness and also links to nature, as all the white elements are natural and give the impression that the swan is a part of nature. White also suggests purity, as if the swan is something pure. However the bird is also part of the world as it has a 'black beak' just like the 'black ledges'. The poet suggests that the swan has gentle, soft elements like 'silk' but is also dangerous: 'knifing'.

— explanation of effect of use of imagery linked to understanding the ideas in the poem

— developed examination of the metaphor with well-chosen evidence

— starting to consider the ways contrast has been demonstrated

Comments on Response 1

This response starts well as the student has shown that they understand the main point of the poem, which means that they can then build their response with evidence. There are some clear selections of evidence to support their interpretation of ideas and the comments on this help to build the response. However, the response focuses very much on particular features and doesn't really develop the ways in which the writer is using particular details to link to an overall idea about life.

4   How could this sample response be improved? Using the middle rung of the Check your progress ladder at the end of this chapter, think about what advice you might give to this student in order to improve their work.

5   Now read the following response to the same task. As you read, think about what the student has done that is an improvement on Response 1, and what advice this student might need in order to make even more progress.

Response 2

The poet uses contrasting imagery of black and white to suggest that the swan is a metaphor for goodness and evil.

Nature imagery such as the whiteness of 'blossom / lilies' are contrasted with 'biting / black / dark / knifing', suggesting that the swan is an elemental force, capable of purity as well as evil.

This is later picked up with the metaphoric use of 'white cross', a symbol for Christianity, suggesting that this bird encapsulates the internal conflict between good and evil in human nature.

The final question returns to the starting question, directly asking whether this experience has caused the reader to look inside and understand the lessons that nature can teach us.

— much clearer hook to the task, showing sophisticated understanding

— evidence used to support interpretation

— convincing interpretation of the metaphor

— interpretation of the effect of structure

Comments on Response 2

A sophisticated reading of the poem with evidence used to support throughout. The student wastes no time before demonstrating a very insightful reading of the poem and uses evidence skilfully to support this reading. The comments on effects of structure are also very well linked to the writer's ideas and purpose.

Check your progress

- I can present a succinct overview of the writer's viewpoints and ideas.
- I can select and analyse significant details from the text in a summative, precise way to support my interpretations.
- I can analyse and evaluate the effects of particular language features in detail, exploring how the writer manipulates language in order to create a range of potential effects on the reader.
- I can analyse and evaluate significant features of form and structure, linking them together to explore how a writer has manipulated them in order to create particular meanings.
- I can use technical vocabulary with confidence and precision.

- I can demonstrate a very clear and thorough understanding of the writer's viewpoints and ideas.
- I can make detailed references to the text to support my interpretation.
- I can select and analyse particular language techniques in detail, linking them precisely to the overall effect being created.
- I can analyse particular features of structure and form in detail, linking them precisely to the overall effect being created.
- I can use technical vocabulary as a precise shorthand to explain effects.

- I can interpret the writer's viewpoints and ideas.
- I can make careful, precise selections of words and phrases to support my interpretations of viewpoints and ideas.
- I can explain and comment in detail on how language techniques are used to communicate ideas to the reader.
- I can comment in detail on the writer's use of structural features, linking these precisely to the overall effect being created.
- I can use accurate technical vocabulary to explain effects.

Chapter 5

Working with context

What's it all about?

In this chapter, you will learn how different types of context can be used to help understand and analyse a range of texts for English Literature. Context should never be seen as separate from a writer's ideas or techniques but as an integral part of both.

In this chapter, you will learn how to

- explore how writers use different settings to develop characters

- explore how writers use different time periods to develop themes and ideas

- explore how ideas about literary context can inform your reading of a text

- apply your skills to an English Literature task.

	English Literature GCSE
Which AOs are covered?	AO3 Show understanding of the relationships between texts and the contexts in which they were written
Where will this be useful?	In your exam, you will be writing about the ways in which writers communicate their ideas and viewpoints to the reader. You will explore ideas about context to help you analyse writers' ideas and techniques in more detail. You will be expected to consider the range of ways different contexts might have affected writers when they wrote texts, how different settings are used and how we might view a text today.

Explore how writers use different settings to develop characters

Learning objectives
You will learn how to
- explore connotations of settings
- link a writer's use of settings to the development of a character.

Assessment objectives
- English Literature AO1, AO2, AO3

How can ideas about a place help you to understand a character?

Getting you thinking

1. What are the similarities and differences between these two pictures?

In her 1984 short story 'The Darkness Out There', Penelope Lively uses stereotypical contexts to show that a character's view of the world is flawed and immature:

- that evil lurks in dark places like woods and forests, which are typical fairy tale settings
- that old ladies who live in quaint country cottages are harmless.

Explore the skills

The main character in 'The Darkness Out There' is a girl called Sandra who is on the verge of adulthood. At the beginning of the story, she is on the way to visit an old lady called Mrs Rutter to help her with some jobs around the house as part of her work for the Good Neighbours Club.

In this extract, Sandra passes the woods at Packer's End.

> When they were small, six and seven and eight, they'd been scared stiff of Packer's End. Then, they hadn't known about the German plane. It was different things then; witches and wolves and tigers. Sometimes they'd go there for a dare, several of them, skittering over the field and into the edge of the trees, giggling and shrieking, not too far in, just far enough for it to be scary, for the branch shapes to look like faces and clawed hands, for the wolves to rustle and creep in the greyness you couldn't quite see into, the clotted shifting depths of the place.
>
> But after, lying on your stomach at home on the hearthrug watching telly with the curtains drawn and the dark shut out, it was cosy to think of Packer's End, where you weren't.
>
> After they were twelve or so the witches and wolves went away. Then it was the German plane. And other things too. You didn't know who there might be around, in woods and places. Like stories in the papers. Girl attacked on lonely road. Police hunt rapist. There was this girl, people at school said, this girl some time back who'd been biking along the field path and these two blokes had come out of Packer's End. They'd had a knife, they'd threatened to carve her up, there wasn't anything she could do, she was at their mercy. People couldn't remember what her name was, exactly, she didn't live round here any more. Two enormous blokes, sort of gypsy types.
>
> Penelope Lively, from 'The Darkness Out There'

Woods and forests are used in many fairy stories to represent fear and evil. Lively uses this familiar context to show Sandra's immaturity at the beginning of the story.

2   List any references to fairy stories you can find.

3   What evidence can you find that Sandra was never really frightened of Packer's End?

4   Are there any suggestions that the story about the girl attacked in Packer's End might not be true?

5   Are there any suggestions that Sandra is more childish than she thinks?

Develop the skills

In this extract, Sandra is inside Mrs Rutter's cottage.

She seemed composed of circles, a cottage-loaf of a woman, with a face below which chins collapsed one into another, a creamy smiling pool of a face in which her eyes snapped and darted.

'Tea, my duck?' she said. 'Tea for the both of you? I'll put us a kettle on.'

The room was stuffy. It had a gaudy lino floor with the pattern rubbed away in front of the sink and round the table; the walls were cluttered with old calendars and pictures torn from magazines; there was a smell of cabbage. The alcove by the fireplace was filled with china ornaments: big-eyed flop-eared rabbits and beribboned kittens and flowery milkmaids and a pair of naked chubby children wearing daisy chains.

The woman hauled herself from a sagging armchair. She glittered at them from the stove, manoeuvring cups, propping herself against the draining-board. 'What's your names, then? Sandra and Kerry. Well, you're a pretty girl, Sandra, aren't you. Pretty as they come. There was – let me see, who was it? – Susie, last week. That's right, Susie.' Her eyes investigated, quick as mice. 'Put your jacket on the back of the door, dear, you won't want to get that messy. Still at school, are you?'

6   Find words and phrases which suggest Mrs Rutter looks like a typical 'old dear'.

7   How does Lively's description of Mrs Rutter's house reinforce this impression of her?

8   Is there anything in the description which suggests Mrs Rutter might not be as harmless as Sandra thinks?

In the following extract, Mrs Rutter tells how she and her sister Dot left a young German airman to die in World War 2.

'He was hurt pretty bad. He was kind of talking to himself. Something about mutter, mutter … Dot said he's not going to last long, and a good job too, three of them that'll be. She'd been a VAD so she knew a bit about casualties, see.' Mrs Rutter licked her lips; she looked across at them, her eyes darting. 'Then we went back to the cottage.'

There was silence. The fire gave a heave and a sigh. 'You what?' said the boy.

'Went back inside. It was bucketing down, cats and dogs.'

The boy and girl sat quite still, on the far side of the table.

'That was eighteen months or so after my hubby didn't come back from Belgium.' Her eyes were on the girl; the girl looked away. 'Tit for tat, I said to Dot.'

After a moment she went on. 'Next morning it was still raining and blow me if the bike hadn't got a puncture. I said to Dot, I'm not walking to the village in this, and that's flat, and Dot was running a bit of a temp, she had the 'flu or something coming on. I tucked her up warm and when I'd done the chores I went back in the wood, to have another look. He must have been a tough so-and-so, that Jerry, he was still mumbling away. It gave me a turn, I can tell you. I'd never imagined he'd last the night. I could see him better, in the day-time; he was bashed up pretty nasty. I'd thought he was an old bloke, too, but he wasn't. He'd have been twentyish, that sort of age.'

The boy's spoon clattered to the floor; he did not move.

'I reckon he may have seen me, not that he was in a state to take much in. He called out something. I thought, oh no, you had this coming to you, mate, there's a war on. You won't know that expression – it was what everybody said in those days. I thought, why should I do anything for you? Nobody did anything for my Bill, did they? I was a widow at thirty-nine. I've been on my own ever since.'

The boy shoved his chair back from the table.

'He must have been a tough bastard, like I said. He was still there that evening, but the next morning he was dead. The weather'd perked up by then and I walked to the village and got a message to the people at Clapton. They were ever so surprised; they didn't know there'd been a Jerry plane come down in the area at all. There were lots of people came to take bits for souvenirs, I had a bit myself but it's got mislaid, you tend to mislay things when you get to my age.'

The boy had got up. He glanced down at the girl. 'I'm going,' he said. 'Dunno about you, but I'm going.'

9 How does Lively's description create sympathy for the young German?

10 How does Lively's description of the way Mrs Rutter tells the story add to the horror of what she did?

11 What differences can you find between the way Sandra and Kerry (the boy) react to the story?

12 In the final extract on the right, Lively describes Sandra's realisation. What has the incident with Mrs Rutter taught Sandra?

Apply the skills

13 Use the evidence you have gathered in answering the previous questions to help you with the following task.

How does Lively use settings to present ideas about growing up in 'The Darkness Out There'?

And she would hear, she thought, always, for a long time anyway, that voice trickling on, that soft old woman's voice; would see a tin painted with cornflowers, pretty china ornaments.

'It makes you want to throw up,' he said. 'Someone like that.'

She couldn't think of anything to say. He had grown; he had got older and larger. His anger eclipsed his acne, the patches of grease on his jeans, his lardy midriff. You could get people all wrong, she realised with alarm. You could get people wrong and there was a darkness that was not the darkness of tree shadows and murky undergrowth and you could not draw the curtains and keep it out because it was in your head, once known, in your head for ever like lines from a song. One moment you were walking in long grass with the sun on your hair and birds singing and the next you glimpsed darkness, an inescapable darkness. The darkness was out there and it was a part of you and you would never be without it, ever.

She walked behind him, through a world grown unreliable, in which flowers sparkle and birds sing but everything is not as it appears, oh no.

14 Before you start the task, look at this response from a student and identify where you feel they have done well and where they might improve.

Lively uses stereotypes of old ladies and country cottages to show Sandra's immaturity. When Sandra first meets Mrs Rutter, she cannot see further than the 'creamy smiling pool of a face'. Also, Mrs Rutter is 'composed of circles': soft, non-threatening shapes. Even at this stage, Sandra does not notice Mrs Rutter's eyes which 'snapped and darted' and were 'quick as mice' suggesting there is more to Mrs Rutter than meets the eye. Instead, Sandra judges based on the typical ornaments you would expect to find in a 'nice' old lady's cottage like 'big-eyed flop-eared rabbits and beribboned kittens'.

— focus on writer straight away establishes clear overview

— context is identified explicitly

— consistently well-chosen evidence embedded in response

— comments on effects of language

Sandra's view of Mrs Rutter as a poor helpless old lady is confirmed when Sandra learns that she lost her husband in the war. Again, Sandra judges too quickly and sees Mrs Rutter as a victim of the cruel and evil Germans. However, Lively shows that this stereotypical view is also wrong. Mrs Rutter and her sister found a young wounded German airman, noticed that he was still alive and calling for his 'mutter' or mother in English and then 'went back inside'. Kerry recognises the cruelty and heartlessness of this action but Sandra is too shocked to speak. Even forty years later, Mrs Rutter feels no remorse or guilt for her actions. Here, Lively has used ideas about good and evil from World War 2 to highlight Sandra's immaturity because she is unable to see beyond the obvious or stereotypical. Also, Lively has used conventions of fairy tales to show Sandra's immaturity. In a way, she and Kerry are like Hansel and Gretel entering the witch's house without recognising the danger. However Kerry, the one she didn't 'reckon much on' is the one who actually saves her.

— sentence links context to ideas and returns to the question

— ideas about literary context

Check your progress:

⬆⬆ I can include ideas about context in a clear overview which focuses sharply on the question in order to analyse and evaluate the effects of language and structure.

⬆ I can use context to help me explore ideas thoroughly and analyse the effects of language and structure.

🔺 I can use context to help me explain ideas and to comment in detail on the language and structure of a text.

Checklist for success

- Stay focused on the question.
- Include some well-selected evidence.
- Analyse the effects of particular words, literary techniques and structural features, linked to the ideas and themes in the text.
- Use ideas about context to help develop your ideas.

Explore how writers use different time periods to develop themes and ideas

Learning objectives
You will learn how to
- explore how the time in which a text is set can develop themes and ideas
- explore how a writer uses language to explore ideas.

Assessment objectives
- English Literature AO1, AO2, AO3

How can understanding a text's historical setting help you to understand its themes and ideas?

Getting you thinking

Read the following information.

The Great Famine

In 1845, Ireland was ruled by the British government. Many Irish farmers were poor and grew potatoes on small farms. In 1845, potato blight severely affected the harvest. The potatoes rotted and could not be eaten, leading to widespread famine and disease that caused around 1 million deaths between 1845 and 1851 and a further million people to emigrate.

Ireland remained a net exporter of food throughout most of the five-year famine. Historian Cecil Woodham-Smith suggests that no issue has provoked so much anger and embittered relations between England and Ireland as 'the indisputable fact that huge quantities of food were exported from Ireland to England throughout the period when the people of Ireland were dying of starvation.'

1 Note down the three most important points in the extract.

Explore the skills

Seamus Heaney's 1966 poem 'At a Potato Digging' considers the potato crop in his native Ireland. In part I, Heaney describes a modern potato harvest.

I

A mechanical digger wrecks the drill,
Spins up a dark shower of roots and mould.
Labourers swarm in behind, stoop to fill
Wicker creels. Fingers go dead in the cold.

Like crows attacking crow-black fields, they stretch
A higgledy line from hedge to headland;
Some pairs keep breaking ragged ranks to fetch
A full creel to the pit and straighten, stand

- only modern words in the poem immediately place description in modern day
- Heaney uses animal imagery to describe the diggers
- regular use of enjambment suggests relentless procession up and down field and monotony of the work

Tall for a moment but soon stumble back
To fish a new load from the crumbled surf.
Heads bow, trucks bend, hands fumble towards the black
Mother. Processional stooping through the turf

Turns work to ritual. Centuries
Of fear and homage to the famine god
Toughen the muscles behind their humbled knees,
Make a seasonal altar of the sod.

— digging is compared to fishing

— semantic field of religious words

2 How does Heaney use language to create a powerful picture of the potato digging in part I? Use the annotations to support your answer. Aim to write at least 200 words.

Develop the skills

In part II, Heaney describes a good harvest.

II

Flint-white, purple. They lie scattered
Like inflated pebbles. Native
to the blank hutch of clay
where the halved seed shot and clotted
these knobbed and slit-eyed tubers seem
the petrified hearts of drills. Split
by the spade, they show white as cream.

Good smells exude from crumbled earth.
The rough bark of humus erupts
knots of potatoes (a clean birth)
whose solid feel, whose wet inside
promises taste of ground and root.
To be piled in pits; live skulls, blind-eyed.

Part III flashes back to 1845, the time of the Great Famine. Notice how Heaney has changed the tense from present to past in this section.

III

Live skulls, blind-eyed, balanced on
wild higgledy skeletons
scoured the land in 'forty-five,'
wolfed the blighted root and died.

The new potato, sound as stone,
putrified when it had lain
three days in the long clay pit.
Millions rotted along with it.

Mouths tightened in, eyes died hard,
faces chilled to a plucked bird.
In a million wicker huts
beaks of famine snipped at guts.

A people hungering from birth,
grubbing, like plants, in the bitch earth,
were grafted with a great sorrow.
Hope rotted like a marrow.

Stinking potatoes fouled the land,
pits turned pus in filthy mounds:
and where potato diggers are
you still smell the running sore.

3 Complete the following table.

Words from part II which describe the good harvest	Words from part III which describe the effects of the potato blight
'White as cream'	'pus in filthy mounds'

4 What is the effect of the repetition of 'live skulls, blind-eyed' across parts II and III?

5 In part III, the lines become shorter and the rhythm becomes faster and more insistent. Why might Heaney have done this?

6 Complete the following table.

Animal/Plant image	Effect
'wolfed the blighted root'	
'faces chilled to a plucked bird'	
'beaks of famine snipped at guts'	
'grubbing, like plants, in the bitch earth'	A strange image: 'grubbing' suggests starving people finding food like insects would. Comparing people to 'plants' suggests their connection to the natural world; the image adds to the dehumanising effect of the famine. The 'black mother' who brought the good harvest is now the 'bitch earth' as nature can deny as well as provide. The word 'bitch' suggests spite and is linked closely to the word 'earth'; both are one syllable with short vowels and harsh 'th' consonant sounds adding to the idea of something spiteful and deliberate.
'hope rotted like a marrow'	

Apply the skills

In part IV, Heaney returns to the present day and describes workers resting for lunch.

IV

Under a white flotilla of gulls
The rhythm deadens, the workers stop.
White bread and tea in bright canfuls
Are served for lunch. Dead-beat, they flop

Down in the ditch and take their fill,
Thankfully breaking timeless fasts;
Then, stretched on the faithless ground, spill
Libations of cold tea, scatter crusts.

Glossary

Libations: pouring out of drink as an offering to a god or in memory of the dead

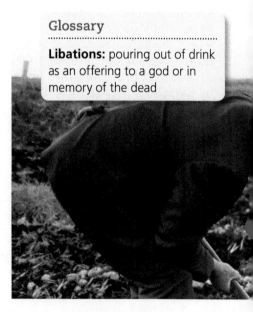

7 How might the phrase, 'dead-beat, they flop down in the ditch' link the modern workers to the farmers of 1845?

8 What is the effect of the religious imagery in part IV? How might it link to the religious imagery in part I?

9 Now you have studied the poem, attempt the following task.

> How does Heaney present the significance of the 'potato digging'?

Read the following response before you start.

> Heaney **1** uses a flashback **2** in part 3 to link the modern 'potato digging' with the terrible events of The Great Famine. **3** He **1** uses nightmare imagery to show that extreme hunger causes desperate, irrational behaviour. Like starving animals, people 'wolfed **4** the blighted root', eating diseased potatoes as there was nothing else. Heaney **1** emphasises the sharp pain of hunger by comparing it to a cruel flock of birds whose 'beaks...snipped at guts'. Heaney **1** uses the idea of a 'running sore', **5** a wound that will not heal, to suggest that The Great Famine will never be forgotten and still causes pain and perhaps anger today. **6** Heaney **1** uses religious imagery in parts 1 and 4 to evoke a sense of irrational fear that, unless the earth is respected, the famine might return. However, 'fear and homage' and 'Libations of cold tea' are pointless as the 'ground' is 'faithless', **5** perhaps suggesting that the 'million' deaths were caused more by economic factors than natural ones.

1 consistent focus on writer as maker of text

2 clear focus on task through comment on structure

3 sentence gives coherent overview and introduces ideas covered later in paragraph

4 good quotation. Could student have said more about 'wolfed'?

5 references to text are well-chosen, embedded and lead to detailed exploration of language

6 excellent question focus. Ideas about context are used cleverly to suggest significance of historical events in modern world

10 This is a very impressive response. Choose two things you think the student has done particularly well and use them as targets for your own writing.

Checklist for success

- Focus closely on Heaney's use of language, structure and other poetic techniques.
- Think about the wider significance of the poem, bearing in mind what you know about the Great Famine.

Check your progress:

- I can include ideas about context in a clear overview which focuses sharply on the question in order to analyse and evaluate the effect of language and structure in a poem.
- I can use context to help me explore ideas thoroughly and analyse the effects of language and structure in a poem.
- I can use context to help me explain ideas and to comment in detail on the language and structure of a poem.

Explore how ideas about literary context can inform your reading of a text

Learning objective
You will learn how to
• explore the *bildungsroman* genre.

Assessment objectives
• English Literature AO1, AO2, AO3

How do writers create authentic childhood narrative voices?

> **Getting you thinking**

1 Look at these words and think about how you might group them:

| judgemental | wise | imaginative | calm | determined |

| persistent | powerless | realistic | honest | naive |

| innocent | tolerant | powerful | passionate | hopeful |

2 **a** Which words do you think carry positive connotations? Which carry negative connotations? Which might be a mixture of both? Use the Venn diagram to place the words where you think they should go.

b Which of these words would you associate with a young person, and which would be more likely to describe an older, wiser person?

Explore the skills

Exploring how a writer uses a particular genre is a way of writing about literary context.

A **bildungsroman** or 'education novel' is a genre of narrative fiction, popular in the nineteenth century. Because *bildungsromans* focus on the emotional development of a character, the narrative voice is usually first person.

Great Expectations by Charles Dickens is a famous *bildungsroman*. In the opening, the **protagonist** Pip reflects on his own youth and innocence.

Key terms

bildungsroman: a genre of narrative fiction where a character develops into emotional maturity via overcoming a series of obstacles and learning some hard lessons about life, themselves, and the right moral path in order to attain wisdom and happiness by the end of the novel

protagonist: the central character of a story

My father's family name being Pirrip, and my Christian name Philip, my infant tongue could make of both names nothing longer or more explicit than Pip. So, I called myself Pip, and came to be called Pip.

I give Pirrip as my father's family name, on the authority of his tombstone and my sister – Mrs Joe Gargery, who married the blacksmith. As I never saw my father or my mother, and never saw any likeness of either of them (for their days were long before the days of photographs), my first fancies regarding what they were like, were unreasonably derived from their tombstones.

Charles Dickens, from *Great Expectations*

3 Which of the words from your list might apply to the young Pip?

4 What do you notice about the narrative style of this novel? Who is telling the story?

Dickens uses the same genre in his novel *David Copperfield*.

I was born at Blunderstone, in Suffolk, or 'there by', as they say in Scotland. I was a posthumous child. My father's eyes had closed upon the light of this world six months, when mine opened on it. There is something strange to me, even now, in the reflection that he never saw me; and something stranger yet in the shadowy remembrance that I have of my first childish associations with his white grave-stone in the churchyard, and of the indefinable compassion I used to feel for it lying out alone there in the dark night, when our little parlour was warm and bright with fire and candle, and the doors of our house were – almost cruelly, it seemed to me sometimes – bolted and locked against it.

Charles Dickens, from *David Copperfield*

5 What similarities can you find between the opening sections of *Great Expectations* and *David Copperfield*? Which words from your list in Activity 1 apply to both Pip and David?

Develop the skills

Although a *bildungsroman* starts with a youthful character, the narrative voice telling the story is actually an adult. They are looking back on their own development into maturity. This means that often the narrative voice is actually more reflective and mature than the younger self they are describing.

In this extract from *David Copperfield*, the young David is punished by his horrible step-father for being unable to learn his lessons.

'Mr. Murdstone! Sir!' I cried to him. 'Don't! Pray don't beat me! I have tried to learn, sir, but I can't learn while you and Miss Murdstone are by. I can't indeed!'

'Can't you, indeed, David?' he said. 'We'll try that.'

He had my head as in a vice, but I twined round him somehow, and stopped him for a moment, entreating him not to beat me. It was only a moment that I stopped him, for he cut me heavily an instant afterwards, and in the same instant I caught the hand with which he held me in my mouth, between my teeth, and bit it through. It sets my teeth on edge to think of it.

He beat me then, as if he would have beaten me to death.

I sat listening for a long while, but there was not a sound. I crawled up from the floor, and saw my face in the glass, so swollen, red, and ugly that it almost frightened me. My stripes were sore and stiff, and made me cry afresh, when I moved; but they were nothing to the guilt I felt. It lay heavier on my breast than if I had been a most atrocious criminal, I dare say.

Long after it was dark I sat there, wondering whether anybody else would come. When this appeared improbable for that night, I undressed, and went to bed; and, there, I began to wonder fearfully what would be done to me. Whether it was a criminal act that I had committed? Whether I should be taken into custody, and sent to prison? Whether I was at all in danger of being hanged?

---

6 Write a paragraph exploring how Dickens portrays David at this point. Does the older narrator give any hints about David's character which suggest he will turn out well in the end?

In this extract from *Jane Eyre* by Charlotte Brontë, the orphan Jane is ten years old and living at Gateshead with her aunt Mrs Reed. Jane has been attacked by her bullying cousin and unfairly locked in a room.

> What a consternation of soul was mine that dreary afternoon! How all my brain was in tumult, and all my heart in insurrection! Yet in what darkness, what dense ignorance, was the mental battle fought! I could not answer the ceaseless inward question – WHY I thus suffered; now, at the distance of – I will not say how many years, I see it clearly.
>
> I was a discord in Gateshead Hall: I was like nobody there; I had nothing in harmony with Mrs. Reed or her children, or her chosen vassalage. If they did not love me, in fact, as little did I love them. They were not bound to regard with affection a thing that could not sympathise with one amongst them; a heterogeneous thing, opposed to them in temperament, in capacity, in propensities; a useless thing, incapable of serving their interest, or adding to their pleasure; a noxious thing, cherishing the germs of indignation at their treatment, of contempt of their judgment. I know that had I been a sanguine, brilliant, careless, exacting, handsome, romping child – though equally dependent and friendless – Mrs. Reed would have endured my presence more complacently; her children would have entertained for me more of the cordiality of fellow-feeling; the servants would have been less prone to make me the scapegoat of the nursery.
>
> Charlotte Brontë, from *Jane Eyre*

 7 **a** What similarities and differences do you notice between the ways David and Jane react to unfair treatment?

b Which character seems to be wiser at this point?

Apply the skills

 8 Before attempting the following task, look back at the list of words in Activity 1 and reread the four extracts.

How do Dickens and Brontë present their young protagonists at the start of the *bildungsroman* novels *David Copperfield*, *Great Expectations* and *Jane Eyre*?

Checklist for success

- Use some of the words from your list to analyse what the reader learns about each young character.
- Use evidence from the extracts to analyse the similarities and differences between the three young characters.

Check your progress:

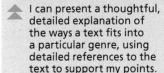

I can explore and analyse the ways in which the text fits the genre with precise supporting details.

I can present a thoughtful, detailed explanation of the ways a text fits into a particular genre, using detailed references to the text to support my points.

I can show clear understanding of the ways a text fits into a particular genre, using evidence from the text to support my points.

Apply your skills to an English Literature task

Learning objectives
You will learn how to
- apply the key skills from this chapter to a new text
- reflect on your progress by looking at different responses to a task.

Assessment objectives
- English Literature AO1, AO2, AO3

Using context to broaden your interpretation of a literary text

In Act 1 of William Shakespeare's play *Hamlet*, the audience learns that Hamlet's father, the King of Denmark, has recently died. Hamlet's uncle Claudius has taken over the throne and married Hamlet's mother, Gertrude. Hamlet is extremely angry about this situation and hates his uncle.

Later, Hamlet meets the ghost of his father who tells him that he was murdered by Claudius and that Hamlet must take revenge by killing Claudius. Hamlet is unable to act on the ghost's orders for most of the play, in part due to moral scruples he cannot overcome.

To think about different ways that different audiences might understand the ghost, you would need to think about:

- the context of production – ideas around at the time the play was written and first performed which may have influenced Shakespeare and Shakespearean audiences

- the context of reception – ideas that audiences at different times might use to help interpret and understand the play but that perhaps didn't exist in Shakespeare's time.

Look at this extract from Act 1 Scene 5 where his father's ghost tells Hamlet who murdered him and asks for revenge.

GHOST	Revenge his foul and most unnatural murder.
HAMLET	Murder!
GHOST	Murder most foul, as in the best it is; But this most foul, strange and unnatural.
HAMLET	Haste me to know't, that I, with wings as swift As meditation or the thoughts of love, May sweep to my revenge.
GHOST	I find thee apt; And duller shouldst thou be than the fat weed That roots itself in ease on Lethe wharf,

Wouldst thou not stir in this. Now, Hamlet, hear
'Tis given out that, sleeping in my orchard,
A serpent stung me; so the whole ear of Denmark
Is by a forged process of my death
Rankly abused: but know, thou noble youth,
The serpent that did sting thy father's life
Now wears his crown.

HAMLET	O my prophetic soul! My uncle!

William Shakespeare, from *Hamlet*

Different audiences might view the inclusion of a ghost as:

- a convention of Revenge Tragedy – Revenge Tragedies were extremely popular in Shakespeare's time and usually featured a ghost who gives the central character a motive for revenge against a powerful and dangerous opponent

- a 'real' event – more people in Shakespeare's time believed in the supernatural than in modern times and therefore, this could be seen as a realistic representation of a possible event

- an insight into Hamlet's unconscious mind: the Ghost could be seen by a modern audience to represent thoughts and feelings of which Hamlet is not aware, following the ideas of psychoanalysis which became popular in the twentieth century.

Psychoanalytic criticism is based on the work of Sigmund Freud in which he separated the human psyche or mind into three parts:

- id – our unconscious wishes and desires, for example, hunger, ambition, sexual desire

- superego – a bit like the conscience or the rules for acceptable behaviour that our parents teach us

- ego – the part of our psyche which contains our conscious awareness of ourselves and our actions. The ego has to mediate between the desires of the id and the rules imposed by the superego.

If we apply this theory to *Hamlet*, we could conclude:

- the ghost represents Hamlet's id or his own unconscious desire to kill his uncle

- Hamlet's superego is represented by his scruples about taking revenge which surface repeatedly

- Hamlet cannot act because his ego is torn between powerful desires for revenge stemming from his id and recognition that murder is wrong, something deeply engrained on his psyche by his superego.

Responding to an English Literature task

1 Now read this practice task and consider how you would respond to it.

Your task
How might an audience respond to the ghost in *Hamlet*?

Checklist for success
A successful response should:

- use ideas about different types of context to broaden your response

- link your ideas about context to the writer's ideas

- link your ideas about context to detailed analysis of language and / or structure and / or form.

Look at this student's response.

Response 1

Shakespeare uses the ghost to introduce the key dilemma of the play to the audience in an exciting and dramatic way. This extract is dramatic because the audience knows it is a revenge tragedy and have been waiting for the ghost to appear since the first scene so Shakespeare has built up tension by leaving the ghost's appearance until the fifth scene. Secondly, the ghost delivers the news in a dramatic way, asking Hamlet to 'revenge his most foul and unnatural murder' but waiting some time before revealing the identity of the murderer as 'the serpent ... that now wears his crown'. The audience might think from Hamlet's response that it is now going to be just a case of how he takes his revenge. 'My prophetic soul' suggests that Hamlet already suspected his uncle and that this will be all the justification he needs to act with 'wings as swift as meditation'. Perhaps the only obstacle will be that Claudius is a powerful and dangerous man which is another feature a Shakespearean audience would expect to find in a revenge tragedy.

- recognition of Shakespeare as the maker of the text
- good idea about dramatic structure
- introducing literary context to develop the idea
- developing the idea further
- good use of embedded quotation throughout
- tentative exploration of effect on audience

Comments on Response 1

This is a good response which starts with a clear focus on Shakespeare as the writer and maker of the text. Evidence is embedded effectively throughout to show a good knowledge and understanding of the text. The student shows understanding of where the extract fits within the play as a whole and can therefore comment effectively on structure. Knowledge of literary context is introduced through the comments about revenge tragedy and this does help to explain possible audience responses. Although evidence is used to show understanding, more could have been made of language and what this reveals about Hamlet's character.

3. How could this sample response be improved? Using the middle rung of the Check your progress ladder at the end of this chapter, think about what advice you might give to this student in order to improve their work.

4. Response 2 is by a different student. As you read, think about what the student has done well.

Response 2

The appearance of a ghost in Act 1 of a revenge tragedy would be
expected by a Shakespearean audience. As expected, the ghost
provides the central dilemma of the play with his demand to 'revenge
his most foul and unnatural murder'. The ghost also reveals that his
murderer now 'wears his crown' setting Hamlet against a formidable
and dangerous opponent, another key feature of a revenge tragedy.
However, many audiences see *Hamlet* as much more than a revenge
tragedy; it can be viewed as a powerful psychological exploration
of the human condition. The ghost is telling Hamlet something
he already suspected as revealed by his comment 'my prophetic
soul' and seems to be giving him a perfect motive to act; a modern
psychoanalytic interpretation could see the ghost as representing
Hamlet's unconscious desire to kill his uncle or what Freud would
have called the id. The id, however, has a balance called the
superego, which is similar to a conscience, and you can already see it
working in this extract. Hamlet says he will take revenge with 'wings
as swift as meditation or thoughts of love', which sounds fast at first.
However, 'meditation' hints at Hamlet's flaw: he thinks too much.
Also 'thoughts of love' is a strange simile to use in this situation as
love and murder are so different. Perhaps Hamlet is unconsciously
revealing that he is happier thinking about love than murder. This
foreshadows the inner conflict which torments Hamlet throughout the
play.

Annotations (right margin):
- reference to literary context
- embedded evidence throughout
- alternative interpretation introduced
- different context of reception explored
- context linked to language analysis
- dramatic structure explored

Comments on Response 2

This is a deeper and more developed response than Response 1.
The student uses literary context when discussing aspects of
revenge tragedy but then develops a discussion about the form
of *Hamlet* by bringing in a different context of reception. Using
information about a psychoanalytic reading of the play then
allows the student to analyse language in an interesting and
original way with discussion of the 'wings' simile. This is then
linked to a perceptive point about structure where the student
cleverly identifies foreshadowing. The whole response is coherent
and uses embedded quotation effectively.

Check your progress

- I can include ideas about context in a clear overview which focuses sharply on the question in order to analyse and evaluate the effects of the language and structure in a text.

- I can explore and analyse the ways in which the text fits the genre with precise supporting details.

- I have a clear overview of how a range of contexts, including contexts of production and reception, can affect texts in a range of ways.

- I can analyse and evaluate ways in which context might influence a writer's themes and ideas.

- I can analyse and evaluate how context can influence a writer's use of language, structure and form.

- I can use the text skilfully, linking my analyses to careful and precise selection of material.

- I can use context to help me explore ideas thoroughly and analyse the effects of language and structure in a text.

- I can present a thoughtful, detailed explanation of the ways a text fits into a particular genre, using detailed references to the text to support my points.

- I can begin to appreciate how a range of contexts, including contexts of production and reception, can affect texts in several ways.

- I can analyse ways in which context can influence a writer's themes and ideas.

- I can analyse how context can influence how a writer uses language, structure and form to create a range of meanings.

- I can link my analyses to well-selected references from the text.

- I can use context to help me explain ideas and to comment in detail on the language and structure of a text.

- I can show clear understanding of the ways a text fits into a particular genre, using evidence from the text to support my points.

- I can understand how a range of contexts, including contexts of production and reception, can affect the shape of a text.

- I can present a detailed explanation of how context can influence a writer's themes and ideas.

- I can present a detailed explanation of how context can influence how a writer uses language, structure and form to create a range of meanings.

- I can use a range of well-selected evidence to support my ideas.

Chapter 6

Forming a critical response

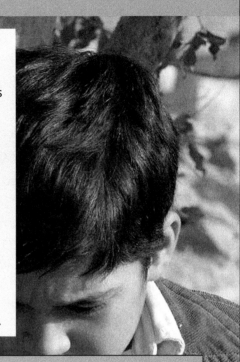

What's it all about?

In this chapter, you will learn how to build longer essay-style responses to unseen and studied texts. You will learn how texts invite different interpretations and how to build on your own comprehension skills and knowledge about analysing language and structure. This type of work is known as a 'critical' response. You will learn how to put those elements together to answer longer essay-style tasks in a convincing evaluative way for English Language and in an analytical way for English Literature, showing the best of all your skills.

In this chapter, you will learn how to

- understand critical reading
- construct a convincing response to literary texts
- construct a convincing response to non-fiction texts
- apply your skills to English Language and English Literature tasks.

	English Language GCSE	English Literature GCSE
Which AOs are covered?	AO4 Evaluate texts critically and support this with appropriate textual references	AO1 Read, understand and respond to texts. Students should be able to maintain a critical style and develop an informed personal response using textual references, including quotations, to support and illustrate interpretations
How will this be tested?	All the texts you will be responding to will be previously unseen. You will be given longer essay-type tasks that expect you to look at significant areas of texts or whole texts and 'evaluate critically'. 'Critical' reading is a step up from basic comprehension questions and expects you to respond to a text in detail, gathering evidence from the text's language, structure or tone and mood. 'Evaluating' means weighing up that evidence to piece together the meaning of the text.	Sometimes you will be responding to a whole play or novel that you have studied in class and sometimes you will be writing about two previously unseen poems. You will be given longer essay tasks that expect you to look at significant areas of texts or whole texts. A 'critical' essay style is a step up from basic comprehension questions and expects you to respond to a text in detail, gathering the evidence in the language, structure and mood.

Understand critical reading

Learning objective

You will learn how to

- explore the nature of criticism and why it is an important part of studying texts.

Assessment objectives

- English Language AO4
- English Literature AO1

How is reading critically different from doing the usual comprehension work?

Getting you thinking

Reviewers have always commented on published works, theatre productions and film in newspapers, magazines and more recently on radio, television or online.

1. Read these two film reviews from broadsheet newspapers of the 2011 film adaptation of Emily Brontë's novel, *Wuthering Heights*.

> From the start, the film sweeps away the period choreography of the conventional literary adaptation, sweeps it away so thoroughly that for the first few minutes I thought that this *Wuthering Heights* must be set a hundred years after a nuclear strike.
>
> Peter Bradshaw, 'Wuthering Heights – review', from *The Guardian*, 10 November 2011

> I'd say this astonishing adaptation of *Wuthering Heights* was one of the most impressive costume dramas I've seen in years, except it's so far removed from any normal expectations of the genre that I'd hesitate to call it a costume drama at all. Andrea Arnold's film certainly boasts the bonnets, romance, shots of the English countryside and 19th-century source material that are the form's hallmarks; but it's also strange, profane and flecked with rime and spittle. It feels, in the best way possible, totally alien.
>
> Robbie Collin, 'Wuthering Heights: review', from *The Telegraph*, 10 November 2011

2. From the reviews above, what different impressions do you get of the film version of *Wuthering Heights*? Do both reviewers seem to 'see' the film in the same way?

Explore the skills

A review is not the only way of presenting a viewpoint on a text. Over time, academics studying English have developed theories about the ways we can understand literary texts.

Like the reviews in Activity 1, their theories show us that there are several ways of reading a text and several ways of interpreting it. This is called **critical reading**.

A piece of writing pulling together all of the evidence for your interpretation is a **critical evaluation**. This would include ideas about:

* the meaning and content of the text and the inferences you can draw from it
* the language and structure of the text and the effects on the reader
* the writer's intentions or possible ideas that they want readers to take away from the text.

Some of the best-known theories are **Marxist** and **feminist** literary theory.

Feminist theory, for example, would always ask precise questions about:

* the role of women in literature
* how women are viewed and presented in texts
* the status of women writers in literary history and the canon.

Read the following extract from the play *Romeo and Juliet* by William Shakespeare, where Lord Capulet is arranging his daughter's marriage without her knowledge. Then answer the questions that feminist theory would be interested in exploring:

CAPULET	Sir Paris, I will make a desperate tender Of my child's love: I think she will be ruled In all respects by me; nay, more, I doubt it not. Wife, go you to her ere you go to bed; Acquaint her here of my son Paris' love; And bid her, mark you me, on Wednesday next – But, soft! what day is this?
PARIS	Monday, my lord,
CAPULET	Monday! ha, ha! Well, Wednesday is too soon, O' Thursday let it be: o' Thursday, tell her, She shall be married to this noble earl. Will you be ready? do you like this haste?

We'll keep no great ado, – a friend or two;
For, hark you, Tybalt being slain so late,
It may be thought we held him carelessly,
Being our kinsman, if we revel much:
Therefore we'll have some half a dozen friends,
And there an end. But what say you to Thursday?

PARIS   My lord, I would that Thursday were to-morrow.

CAPULET   Well get you gone: o' Thursday be it, then.

Go you to Juliet ere you go to bed, Prepare her, wife, against this wedding-day.

William Shakespeare, from *Romeo and Juliet*

3

a What do you notice about Capulet's use of the first-person pronouns, 'I', 'my', 'me'?

b What do you notice about the way Capulet addresses his wife and how he asks her to inform Juliet of her future marriage?

c What is the impact of the modal verbs, 'She *will* be ruled', 'She *shall* be married'?

One of the most important skills to enable you to read critically is the ability to ask precise and meaningful questions to help you investigate texts.

4 Think of two more questions it might be important to ask if you were considering how women are presented in the extract.

Develop the skills

Marxist theory:

- considers that literature reflects the time in which it was written and gives us important clues about society, particularly in terms of who holds the power in society

- considers the role that social class plays in the characters and themes of texts, particularly in terms of which social classes may be oppressed and which may be the oppressors

- considers how the context of the text reflects a writer's themes and ideas.

A Marxist **interpretation** of a text would always ask questions about those issues.

Read the following extract from *Love on the Dole* by Walter Greenwood. The novel is set in Salford during the 1930s when a great depression meant that many of the working classes were suffering from the effects of unemployment.

> It got you slowly, with the slippered stealth of an unsuspected, malignant disease.
>
> You got into the habit of slouching, of putting your hands into your pockets and keeping them there; of glancing at people, furtively, ashamed of your secret, until you fancied that everybody eyed you with suspicion. You knew that your shabbiness betrayed you; it was apparent for all to see. You prayed for the winter evenings and kindly darkness. Darkness, poverty's cloak. Breeches backside patched and repatched; patches on knees, on elbows. Jesus! All bloody patches. Gor' blimey!
>
> [...]
>
> Round Trafford Park and to all the other engineering shops: 'Any chance of a job, mister?'

Key term

interpretation: a particular way of looking at or understanding something

— What is implied by the phrase, 'an unsuspected, malignant disease'?

— What do the references to 'furtively' and 'suspicion' suggest about the way the unemployed narrator is made to feel?

— What does using the 'voice' of the unemployed narrator add to the depiction of the unemployed?

> 'No.'
>
> 'Any vacancies, mate?'
>
> Snappily: 'Get off, out of it. Open y' eyes,' a thumb jerked ——— towards a board: NO HANDS WANTED.
>
> Trudging home, dispirited, tired. Pausing on Trafford Bridge to stare at the ships in the Ship Canal. ———
>
> [...]
>
> Nothing to do with time; nothing to spend; nothing to do tomorrow nor the day after; nothing to wear; can't get married. A living corpse; a unit of the spectral army of three million lost ——— men.
>
> Walter Greenwood, from *Love on the Dole*

What is implied here about the attitudes of others towards the unemployed?

What might the writer be implying about the impact of industrialisation by making reference to the Ship Canal?

By using this image, what else is implied about the role of working class men in an unequal society?

5 Answer the questions in the annotations that a Marxist critic would be interested in exploring.

6 Think of two additional questions a Marxist critic might want to ask about:

a the writer's use of language

b the writer's tone.

In evaluating a text in the way a critic would, you need to:

- ask questions about what else you see in the text that may not have been in the writer's mind when they wrote the text
- ask precise questions about the writer's use of language, structure and tone
- present your response – your interpretation – in an essay style.

Apply the skills

7 Using some of the ideas that you have already noted, complete the following task.

Choose one of the texts you have studied in this section and write 2–3 paragraphs explaining your ideas on either:

how William Shakespeare presents women in this extract

or

how Walter Greenwood presents the unemployed working classes in this extract.

Check your progress:

I can read texts, ask precise questions and form an interpretation for myself.

I can understand that by asking particular types of questions it is possible to form an interpretation of a text.

I can understand that there is more than one way to read and interpret a text.

Construct a convincing response to literary texts

Learning objective
You will learn how to
• understand how to put your interpretation together clearly and effectively.

Assessment objectives
• English Language AO4
• English Literature AO1

You have gathered ideas about a text – how do you put it all together?

Getting you thinking

Look at the following task.

> Write a critical evaluation of the poem 'The Tyger', exploring how the poet William Blake presents ideas about the power of man versus nature.

 1 **a** What are the key words in the task?

b What words in particular give you a clue as to how to interpret the text's meaning and ideas?

Critical evaluation means you need to decide what your interpretation of the text might be.

You would construct this by:

• using your comprehension skills
• using your language skills
• using your structure skills
• working out the mood or tone of the text
• working out the poet's possible intentions or messages.

Explore the skills

Your first step is to gather and organise your ideas.

A student has been working on the first two stanzas of the poem 'The Tyger', and highlighted different aspects in different colours to help them organise their ideas:

language ideas   structure ideas   mood ideas   ideas about the poet's message.

Read the first two stanzas through twice. Then look at the student's notes.

> Tyger Tyger, burning bright,
> In the forests of the night;
> What immortal hand or eye,
> Could frame thy fearful symmetry?
>
> In what distant deeps or skies.
> Burnt the fire of thine eyes?
> On what wings dare he aspire?
> What the hand, dare seize the fire?
>
> And what shoulder, & what art,
> Could twist the sinews of thy heart?
> And when thy heart began to beat,
> What dread hand? & what dread feet?

ideas about the poet's message: A lot of references to the body – physical labour – is this about making something or destroying it? Written during Industrial Revolution – ideas about 'daring' and 'aspiration' – is the tiger a metaphor for what man has created/is creating? Does man believe he is godlike?

structure ideas: very regular rhyme scheme – rhyming couplets – regular mechanical (?) rhythm. Repeats 'what' – all 3 stanzas are made up of questions – why? What is Blake trying to understand?

mood ideas: Has an atmosphere of 'fear' and 'dread' – idea of the dark forest – the mood seems dark/ foreboding – like a warning.

language ideas 'immortal hand' sounds like something godlike but no reference to God – important? 'fearful symmetry' doesn't sound natural – describing the shape of the tiger and his form? Could the tiger be a metaphor? A lot of references to fire and burning – ideas about destruction.

2 Now read the rest of the poem and use the annotations to help you make notes in a similar style to the student above.

> What the hammer? what the chain,
> In what furnace was thy brain?
> What the anvil? what dread grasp,
> Dare its deadly terrors clasp!
>
> When the stars threw down their spears
> And water'd heaven with their tears:
> Did he smile his work to see?
> Did he who made the Lamb make thee?
>
> Tyger Tyger burning bright,
> In the forests of the night:
> What immortal hand or eye,
> Dare frame thy fearful symmetry?
>
> William Blake, from 'The Tyger'

What semantic field is Blake using by referring to 'hammer', 'chain', 'anvil' and 'furnace'? How could this be an important link to the context of the poem?

What is emotive about this image and what message is Blake trying to convey about nature's reaction to 'the tyger'?

Who is being referred to here? Can you think of a reason why the Lamb is referred to?

What do you notice about the rhythm and rhyme scheme of the poem? Could this be a deliberate choice? What could it represent?

What effect or impact does the repetition of this verse have?

3 Now look back at the whole poem and use the student's initial thoughts and questions, as well as your own, to compile your own more detailed notes to shape into your critical essay. You could do this in a series of spider diagrams or a chart.

Develop the skills

Your next step is to *shape an argument* about the text you are studying. To do this, you need a clear viewpoint on the text. It can be useful to begin with a **defining statement** on which to base your argument. For example:

> Write a critical evaluation of the poem 'The Tyger', exploring how the poet William Blake presents the power of man versus nature.

> <u>Defining statement</u>
>
> My interpretation: Blake is highlighting how man is behaving like God, but that his creations are powerful and dangerous, like a wild predator, causing the natural world to be fearful and in despair.

4 Write one more defining statement that you could base an interpretation of the poem on.

5 The next step is *selection*:

   a Which points in your notes and planning seem key or most important to help present your argument?

   b Which ones link most logically to your defining statement?

   c Decide which points you would like to keep and use in your response and which, if any, you would like to reject.

Once all of your ideas are selected, gathered and organised, get straight into answering the question. Don't waste time on lengthy introductions or passages about the context or the author.

Look at this possible opening to the task.

> Blake's poem 'The Tyger' uses the idea of a wild, predatory, hungry animal as a metaphor for the creation of the Industrial society that he was witnessing. This creation was the work of men – who were amassing great power and wealth – at the expense of the natural world. The tyger is presented as being powerful and terrible and Blake questions how such a force for destruction can exist in nature and be the work of an 'immortal' hand. This leads us to consider how similar forces for destruction can exist as a result of man's desire for power.

6 a How does it link clearly to the question?

   b How does it use the text in a skilful way to link to the defining statement?

   c Write another paragraph linking one of your language points to the overall mood of the poem:

   • Make sure it adds to the argument.

   • Make sure it sticks to the question.

Look at this possible concluding paragraph.

> It would seem that, overall, the poet is giving a strong message about man's arrogance and that he feels he has godlike powers and abilities. Blake's message seems to be aimed at the wealthy industrialists of the age, who are harnessing the powers of nature – land, coal, water, the labour of the working class – to build their industrial empires and their wealth. Blake's constant questioning in the poem suggests that society itself should be questioning the danger of these actions and he leaves us with a stanza that repeats his opening warning thoughts. This creates not only a cyclical structure in the poem, but warns us against the past, how man's arrogance has led to fallen empires before. It also warns us about the future and as our world becomes ever more polluted and industrialised, we are reminded of the danger we are in as predatory consumerism seeks to destroy our planet.

 7 **a** How does this effectively bring together the interpretation of the poem we saw in the defining statement in Activity 4?

b How does it use contextual knowledge effectively and subtly?

Apply the skills

8 You will now build on the work that you have done earlier to complete the following task.

For your critical evaluation of 'The Tyger':

a continue your opening paragraph on language and mood

b then go on to write the middle section of the essay, this time linking the structure of the poem with some of Blake's key ideas and messages

c finish your section in a way that links seamlessly with the conclusion above.

Checklist for success
- Look for the clues the writer has left behind.
- Ask questions.
- Make your deductions or inferences.
- Present your ideas as clear statements.
- Use quotations from the text to support those ideas, in sophisticated ways.
- Explain the inferences you have made to reach your interpretation.

Check your progress:

 I can gather and organise perceptive ideas to present a convincing and compelling argument for my original interpretation.

 I can gather and organise my ideas to present a convincing interpretation of the text.

 I can plan, write and support a response to a text which shows my own interpretation of the text.

Construct a convincing response to non-fiction texts

Learning objective
You will learn to
• understand how to put your evidence together clearly and effectively for non-fiction texts.

Assessment objectives
• English Language AO4
• English Literature AO1

You are confident when presenting your ideas about poems and stories, but you find it harder with non-fiction texts. How do you improve?

Getting you thinking

Writing about different types of texts in a critically evaluative way is a skill – but there is a method to it that you can learn and practise.

The same skills you use for evaluating literary texts apply to non-literary ones too. They involve:

Skill 1 using your comprehension, language, and structure skills to work out the viewpoint or key message(s) of the text

Skill 2 working out the tone of the text to understand the writer's attitude or feelings

Skill 3 deciding on your interpretation of the text in order to present your evaluation in a convincing and compelling way.

A convincing interpretation is one that will definitely persuade your reader that your interpretation is valid and well argued.

A compelling interpretation will leave your reader in no doubt about your interpretation of the text you are writing about as it will be so strongly argued.

1 Look at the following task and think about how you might tackle it.

Write a critical evaluation exploring how Jean Sprackland has presented the unusual event that occurs on her walk on the beach.

2 **a** Which words in the task are asking you to demonstrate Skill 1 above?

b Which aspect of the task suggests the writer is going to show you her feelings or attitudes about something?

Explore the skills

You are going to look at a complete text and practise the skills learned in 6.2. This time however, you are looking at a non-fiction text.

Read the following extract from the book *Strands* by Jean Sprackland. She describes walking on her local beach and encountering an unusual event.

This time you have colour-coded questions to help you think about the writer's:

- language
- structure
- tone
- key messages

When I was a child, it was said to be lucky to have a ladybird land on your sleeve. My dad certainly liked it when they visited the garden, because they ate the greenfly that plagued his raspberry canes. There was an air of mild enchantment carried by the single ladybird – the one that chose you and rested on you, perhaps just for a minute or two, before unfolding itself and flying away home. [...]

One muggy August day, there is a phenomenal swarm of seven-spot ladybirds on this coast. Millions of them divert onshore, interrupting their journey from who-knows-where, [...] They're bizarrely out of place on the beach. They fill the air, and seagulls make slow predatory circles overhead. They blunder drunkenly on the ground, turning the sand red. They drip from fence posts and pool underneath.

We walk on the beach with our faces covered in scarves, though it's midsummer. Still they land on our eyelids and in our hair, and tumble ticklishly down inside our clothes. As we walk, they crunch underfoot; they're everywhere, [...] Families abandon their picnics and flee. People lock themselves inside their cars. [...]

These childhood gifts, these small enchantments, are suddenly so extravagantly numerous that their currency has collapsed. They've become worthless, and worse than worthless. Now they look like tiny curses.

[...]

What is it about swarms that raises the hair on the back of our necks? Ladybirds are not harmful: they don't sting like wasps, and they don't devastate crops like locusts. But it seems we can have too much of a good thing. A sudden onslaught on this scale feels threatening; it feels like a plague. Things are out of kilter. What does it mean? What will come next? Is it an omen of some kind; a judgement on us? [...] 'Ladybird Books,' laughs my friend. 'Remember their slogan? *Everybody loves a ....*' He stops abruptly and spits one out. The beach is almost deserted by now, and this is starting to feel apocalyptic.

A dog walker coming the other way calls out: 'Aren't they horrible little bastards?' And he breaks into a run.

Jean Sprackland, from *Strands*

 a Investigate language by making notes about:
- the different ways the words 'plagued' and 'plague' are used
- the sound qualities of the words 'blunder', 'drip' and 'crunch' and their connotations
- the impression that's created by 'tumble ticklishly'
- the contrast between 'small enchantments' and 'horrible little bastards'.

b Investigate structure by making notes about:
- how the writer chooses to open and close the anecdote
- how 'One muggy day' shifts the time
- what impression you get from four sentences beginning with 'They'
- the use of simple sentences
- the use of questioning
- the use of dialogue.

c Investigate tone by making notes about:
- how the atmosphere changes from 'There was an air of... ' to 'phenomenal swarm'
- how the writer makes the tone more sinister through the rhetorical question 'What is it...?'
- how the writer relieves the tension towards the end.

d Investigate key messages by making notes about:
- how the writer changes the perception of the ladybird
- how the writer flags up strange happenings in nature 'out of place', 'out of kilter'
- how the ladybird swarm could be a metaphor for other things 'their currency has collapsed', 'too much of a good thing', 'apocalyptic'.

Develop the skills

4 Think back to what you learned in 6.2 about creating a *defining statement* to help you shape your argument. Here are some possible statements to support different interpretations. Which one do you find the most useful? Choose one on which to base your own interpretation or, if you prefer, construct your own.

a Jean Sprackland flags up that something that was once beautiful, simple and innocent can turn into a nightmare.

b Jean Sprackland's writing suggests that the environment is constantly being damaged and that this is making the natural world a potential threat to humans.

c Jean Sprackland's anecdote is like a metaphor for human greed – producing too much or more than we need can have devastating consequences.

5 Now *select and gather* the evidence you would like to use in your response to the task in a grid similar to the one below. Remember to select the points that will most usefully support the *defining statement* of your argument.

a Language points	b Structure points	c Points about tone	d Key messages

It is very important to make a *strong start* which shows you are:
- dealing directly with the question
- setting up a convincing argument for your interpretation.

6 Write up the first half of your response using your language and tone points to aid your interpretation.

The following example shows how a student using defining statement b from Activity 4 began their introduction.

> Jean Sprackland begins this extract with a beautiful, childhood anecdote about ladybirds. It has the effect of reminding readers how beautiful and fragile these creatures are when she describes them as having a 'mild enchantment' about them. They are seen as good, positive creatures for the environment as they consume the 'plague' of greenfly that attacked her father's plants; however the tone changes when...

Apply the skills

7 Now pull all of your earlier responses together in order to complete the following task.

> Write a critical evaluation of how Jean Sprackland has presented the unusual event that occurs on her walk on the beach.

Link your points about language, structure and tone with what you feel are the writer's key messages.

Your concluding paragraph should explain what you feel are Sprackland's key messages for you as a reader and how you feel about the experience she shares with us.

The following example shows how a student using defining statement c from Activity 4 began their conclusion.

> Jean Sprackland paints a clear picture for us of what happens when we have 'too much of a good thing', whether that's possessions, wealth or using the world's natural resources. Her beautiful anecdote of the single 'lucky' ladybird reminds me of how precious some things are before we come to take them for granted...

Check your progress:

▲▲ I can gather and organise perceptive ideas to present a convincing and compelling argument for my original interpretation.

▲▲ I can gather and organise my ideas to present a convincing interpretation of the text.

▲ I can plan, write and support a response to a non-fiction text which shows my own convincing interpretation.

Checklist for success

• Look for the clues the writer has left behind.
• Ask questions.
• Make your deductions or inferences.
• Present your ideas as clear statements.
• Use quotations from the text to support those ideas.
• Explain the inferences you have made to reach your interpretation.

Apply your skills to English Language and English Literature tasks

Learning objectives
You will learn how to
- apply the key skills from this chapter to one unseen English Language task
- apply the key skills from this chapter to one English Literature task
- reflect on your progress through looking at different responses to both tasks.

Assessment objectives
- English Language AO4
- English Literature AO1

Responding to an English Language task

The following extract is from *The Kite Runner* by Khaled Hosseini. Amir is a twelve-year-old boy whose best friend, Hassan, is the son of his father's servant. Through reading to Hassan, Amir makes a discovery about himself. The story is set in Afghanistan.

1 As you read, think about the following questions:
  a What is this extract about?
  b What are we learning about?
  c How has the writer used language, narrative technique and an interesting structure to communicate ideas to the reader?

> Sitting cross-legged, sunlight and shadows of pomegranate leaves dancing on his face, Hassan absently plucked blades of grass from the ground as I read him stories he couldn't read for himself. That Hassan would grow up illiterate […] had been decided the minute he had been born, perhaps even the moment he had been conceived […] – after all, what use did a servant have for the written word? But despite his illiteracy, or maybe because of it, Hassan was drawn to the mystery of words, seduced by a secret world forbidden to him. I read him poems and stories, sometimes riddles – though I stopped reading him those when I saw he was far better at solving them than I was.
> […]
> One day I played a little trick on Hassan. I was reading to him, and suddenly I strayed from the written story. I pretended I was reading from the book, flipping pages regularly, but I had abandoned the text altogether, taken over the story, and made up my own. Hassan, of course, was oblivious to this. To him, the words on the page were a scramble of codes, indecipherable, mysterious. Words were secret doorways and I held all the keys. After, I started to ask him if he liked the story, a giggle rising in my throat, when Hassan began to clap.
> 'What are you doing?' I said.
> 'That was the best story you've read me in a long time,' he said, still clapping.
> I laughed. 'Really?'
> 'Really.'
> 'That's fascinating,' I muttered. I meant it too. This was… wholly unexpected. 'Are you sure, Hassan?'
> He was still clapping. 'It was great, Amir. Will you read me more of it tomorrow?'

[...]

I gave him a friendly shove. Smiled. 'You're a prince, Hassan. You're a prince and I love you.'

That same night, I wrote my first short story. It took me thirty minutes. It was a dark little tale about a man who found a magic cup and learned that if he wept into the cup, his tears were turned into pearls. But even though he had always been poor, he was a happy man and rarely shed a tear. So he found ways to make himself sad so that his tears could make him rich. As the pearls piled up, so did his greed grow. The story ended with the man sitting on a mountain of pearls, knife in hand, weeping helplessly into the cup with his beloved wife's slain body in his arms.

That evening, I climbed the stairs and walked into Baba's smoking room, in my hands the two sheets of paper on which I had scribbled the story. [...]

'What is it, Amir?' Baba said reclining on the sofa and lacing his hands behind his head. Blue smoke swirled around his face. His glare made my throat feel dry. I cleared it and told him I'd written a story. Baba nodded and gave a thin smile that conveyed little more than feigned interest. 'Well, that's very good, isn't it?' he said. Then nothing more. He just looked at me through the cloud of smoke.

I probably stood there for under a minute, but, to this day, it was one of the longest moments of my life. Seconds plodded by, each separated from the next by an eternity. Air grew heavy, damp, almost solid. I was breathing bricks. Baba went on staring me down, and didn't offer to read.

Khaled Hosseini, from *The Kite Runner*

2 Now look at this practice task and consider how you would respond to it.

Your task

Through his friendship with Hassan, the narrator learns an important lesson about his own life. To what extent do you agree?

Checklist for success

In your response you should:

- consider your own impressions of the narrator, the other two characters and Amir's story
- evaluate the effects the characters and story have on you
- support your opinions with quotations from the text.

Reflecting on your progress

3 Read the following response, thinking about what the student has done well and what advice they might need in order to make more progress.

Response 1

The narrator, Amir, learns a lot from spending time with Hassan even though he is the one who seems like he is more superior. The writer uses a rhetorical question 'what use did a servant have for the written word?' to show the difference in their status. **1** Amir can also be mean to Hassan, he stops reading him riddles when he suspects Hassan is 'better at solving them than I was' and plays a 'little trick' on him. **2** It seems like Amir's knowledge makes him superior and the writer uses a metaphor, 'Words were secret doorways', to show how on the surface Hassan seems cleverer. **1**

The story that Amir writes within the story is like a metaphor for the difference between Hassan and himself. **4** The poor man in the story is happy, like Hassan is genuinely happy with Amir's storytelling. But, by becoming rich, he loses what is precious to him and he has to be miserable to be rich. **2**

Amir doesn't seem miserable, but he can be mean and jealous and he clearly does not have a happy relationship with his father, despite being materially better off than Hassan. **5** He describes how his father has a 'thin smile' and only 'feigned interest' in his story. Amir seems to learn that a servant can make him feel much more valued, **3** saying 'You're a prince, Hassan', than his own father who 'didn't offer to read' the story he was so proud of.

1 makes clear references to language features and gives examples and clear effects

2 has picked up on the key ideas about rich and poor and the difference between Hassan and Amir's social status

3 makes a brief reference to one of the structurally interesting parts of the text

4 makes a perceptive inference here

5 uses embedded quotation and good selections to present ideas about character

Comments on Response 1

This response focuses on the task in a very clear way. It has a clear focus on the language of the extract, though does not develop the comments on effect or link them to the task. It explores some of the key ideas, making clear and very relevant interpretations of some of the ideas in the story about social class and Amir's relationships, one of which is perceptive. The response briefly mentions structure by referring to the story within the story but does not develop this. The answer uses well-chosen quotations from the text and embeds them within the answer.

4 How could this sample response be improved? Using the middle rung of the Check your progress ladder at the end of this chapter, think about what advice you might give to this student in order to improve their work.

5 Now read Response 2. As you read, think about what the student has done that is an improvement on Response 1.

Response 2

The narrator describes Hassan as sitting in 'sunlight and shadows', a metaphor perhaps for their friendship and the way the relationship impacts on both of them. **1** Hassan has the 'sunshine' of listening to Amir read, but also the 'shadows' of being unaware of Amir's somewhat mean tricks on him. These seem to represent a hint of jealousy from Amir, that although he is, on the surface, much better off, he begrudges the fact that Hassan is 'better at solving' riddles than he is. **2** Because of that he actively prevents him from showing this talent by not reading them – this could be a metaphor for the way the rich and powerful prevent the poor from improving their social status – by refusing them access to education and knowledge – keeping the 'scramble of codes' to themselves. **3**

Amir's story has a surprising outcome – it shows his talent to Hassan – and instead of being mean, Hassan is generous and gives praise and applause. **4** He shows he is the better person for his genuine response. Amir is also genuinely taken aback and this is shown in the way the writer uses the simple, innocent dialogue between the boys.

Hassan's act of kindness and praise is the encouragement Amir needs to write his story within the story **4** – an allegorical story which has a simple moral – that riches do not necessarily lead to happiness. **5** This seems almost like an issue from Amir's subconscious as we are able to compare Hassan's contentedness, 'Sitting cross-legged', 'still clapping' with Amir's discomfort in the presence of his father, 'I was breathing bricks'. Amir's relationship with his father, disinterested in his son and his talents, offering no encouragement, 'didn't offer to read', is in sharp contrast to Hassan's response. Hassan teaches Amir the value of encouragement, honesty and the love of friends. **4**

1 makes a subtle, original and perceptive inference to open the response

2 uses embedded quotations judiciously

3 a very perceptive inference linked to social contexts

4 links all of the paragraphs and the conclusion to the task and makes subtle links between paragraphs

5 deals with Amir's story in a concise way

Comments on Response 2

This is a very perceptive and detailed response, which ranges around the text and uses textual support judiciously. It contains a number of extremely strong inferences with some perceptive and mature ideas. Language is dealt with in a subtle way and examinations of metaphor and the structure of the text is blended into the argument. Every paragraph is linked seamlessly and makes direct reference to the question, leading to a strong conclusion.

Responding to an English Literature task

1 Read the following poem, 'The Convergence of the Twain'
by Thomas Hardy. As you read, think about the following
questions:

   a What is this poem about?

   b What ideas do you think the writer is communicating?

   c What do you notice about the ways language and structure
have been used to communicate those ideas to the reader?

The Convergence of the Twain

     In a solitude of the sea
     Deep from human vanity,
And the Pride of Life that planned her, stilly couches she.

     Steel chambers, late the pyres
     Of her salamandrine fires,
Cold currents third, and turn to rhythmic tidal lyres.

     Over the mirrors meant
     To glass the opulent
The sea-worm crawls – grotesque, slimed, dumb, indifferent.

     Jewels in joy designed
     To ravish the sensuous mind
Lie lightless, all their sparkles bleared and black and blind.

     Dim moon-eyed fishes near
     Gaze at the gilded gear
And query: 'What does this vaingloriousness down here?' …

     Well: while was fashioning
     This creature of cleaving wing,
The Imminent Will that stirs and urges everything

     Prepared a sinister mate
     For her – so gaily great –
A Shape of Ice, for the time far and dissociate

     And as the smart ship grew
     In stature, grace and hue,
In shadowy silent distance grew the iceberg too.

     Alien they seemed to be:
     No mortal eye could see
The intimate welding of their later history,

     Or sign that they were bent
     By paths coincident
On being anon twin halves of one august event,

     Till the Spinner of the Years
     Said 'Now!' And each one hears,
And consummation comes, and jars two hemispheres.

Thomas Hardy

2 Now look at this practice task and consider how you would respond to it.

Your task

How does the writer present ideas about the tragedy of the sinking of the *Titanic* in the poem? Refer closely to details from the poem in your answer.

Checklist for success

A successful response should:

- demonstrate your understanding and inferences about the writer's ideas
- include some well-selected evidence
- analyse the effects of particular words, literary techniques and structural features, linked to those ideas.

Reflecting on your progress

3   Read the following response, thinking about what the student has done well and what advice they might need in order to make more progress.

Response 1

Hardy's poem presents the ship *Titanic* as being isolated and lost, away from the 'human vanity' that created her. **1** The first four stanzas are all about the ship. **2** They tell how it was designed with references to its amazing engineering and beautiful decorations, 'steel chambers', 'the mirrors meant to glass the opulent'. **4** Even though the ship is at the bottom of the sea, Hardy tells us what it was like and all that was special about it.

This now seems futile, however, as the only audience for its treasures and engineering are 'dim moon-eyed fishes'. Ironically, the fishes question the 'human vanity' and pride that went into the ship, 'What does this vaingloriousness down here?' **1**

Hardy shifts the topic with the use of 'Well:' and goes on to describe the past. He mirrors the building of the ship with the creation of the ice that destroyed her and uses a regular rhyme scheme, 'grew', 'hue', 'too' perhaps to sound like a ticking time bomb waiting for the 'Now' of fate. **2** This exclamation mirrors the shock that the tragedy caused and the phrase 'jars two hemispheres' suggests it affected the whole world. **3**

1 makes a number of clear inferences, which become more sophisticated as we work through

2 uses relevant quotations throughout

3 makes a sensible point about structure in the first paragraph, but goes on to explore structure in a more detailed way in the third paragraph

4 comments on the use of particular sentence functions

Comments on Response 1

This is a very clear and sensible response, which begins to interpret the text in a sound manner. There are well-chosen quotations used to support the ideas. There are some good ideas about structure, though not as much emphasis on language. Some sentences end abruptly and don't lead the argument forward. The idea of the ticking time bomb is very apt and leads to an idea which could have been developed.

4   How could this sample response be improved? Using the middle rung of the Check your progress ladder at the end of this chapter, think about what advice you might give to this student in order to improve their work.

5   Now read Response 2. As you read, think about what the student has done that is an improvement on Response 1.

Response 2

Hardy presents the ship Titanic as a tragic heroine, referring to the ship in a gendered way as 'she' and describing the ship as alluring using words such as 'ravish' and 'sensuous'. He presents this beautiful creation as heading towards a tragic marriage with a brooding and destructive partner, 'far and dissociate' **1** and brings this idea together in the final stanza when there is an 'intimate welding' between the ship and the iceberg — a 'consummation'. **2**

Hardy's structure of two short lines and one long and the regular repetitive pattern of the rhyme in each stanza, perhaps reflects the ebb and flow of the waters over Titanic as she is now displayed only for the 'dim moon-eyed fishes'. **3** They are presented as having more ability to question the symbol of vanity than mankind did and mankind is made to look foolish in comparison as all the supposed beauty he has created 'to glass the opulent' is now home to the 'grotesque' sea worm. **4**

Hardy uses a proper noun to present the 'Pride of Life' as self important and yet later on reduces the 'mortal eye' to a common noun — again made small against the greater 'Imminent Will' who decided Titanic's fate. **5**

1 judicious and creative use of textual details and quotations embedded into the response

2 begins with an interesting and perceptive idea, which blends into some language analysis and gives a strong overview of the text

3 thoughtful comments on structure

4 extends another original idea and uses the text judiciously to support

5 makes a perceptive language point linked to the focus of the argument

Comments on Response 2

A perceptive and well-argued response which ranges around the poem and makes a very convincing interpretation of the text. The extended idea of the ship as tragic heroine is sophisticated and shows a mature understanding of the text. The ideas flow seamlessly and there is some confident use of subject terminology. Textual references and quotations are used to good effect and the clarity of the expression is exceptionally good.

Check your progress

- I can read texts, ask precise questions and form an interpretation for myself.
- I can gather and organise perceptive ideas to present a convincing and compelling argument for my original interpretation of literary texts.
- I can gather and organise perceptive ideas to present a convincing and compelling argument for my original interpretation of non-fiction texts.

- I can understand that by asking particular types of questions it is possible to form my own interpretation of a text.
- I can gather and organise my ideas to present a convincing interpretation of a literary text.
- I can gather and organise my ideas to present a convincing interpretation of a non-fiction text.

- I can understand that there is more than one way to read and interpret a text.
- I can plan, write and support a response to a literary text which shows my own interpretation.
- I can plan, write and support a response to a non-fiction text which shows my own interpretation.

Chapter 7

Comparing texts

What's it all about?

In this chapter, you will learn to make detailed analytical comparisons between texts by considering ideas, meanings and viewpoints. You will develop ways of forming analytical comparisons between the ways these meanings are conveyed to the reader.

In this chapter, you will learn how to

- compare how writers use tone to convey viewpoints and perspectives
- compare the influence of poetic voices over time
- compare and evaluate how writers explore similar ideas in poetry
- apply your skills to English Language and English Literature tasks.

	English Language GCSE	English Literature GCSE
Which AOs are covered?	AO3 Compare writers' ideas and perspectives, as well as how these are conveyed, across two or more texts	AO2 Analyse the language and methods used by a writer to achieve specific purposes and effects, using relevant subject terminology where appropriate
How will this be tested?	You will be asked to compare viewpoints in two texts and also to think about the ways these viewpoints have been presented. All the texts you will be responding to will be previously unseen.	When you make comparisons between poems, you will be considering the ideas being communicated and also the language, structure and form of the poems. Sometimes you will be responding to poems that you have studied in class and sometimes you will be writing about two previously unseen poems.

Compare how writers use tone to convey viewpoints and perspectives

Learning objective
You will learn how to
- analyse and compare how writers create humour and irony in travel writing from two centuries.

Assessment objective
- English Language AO3

What is irony and how do writers use it for humorous effect?

Getting you thinking

A useful definition of irony is a 'gap' or 'distance' between what is said and what is meant, or what happens and what is meant to happen.

Think about this example:

> 'She broke her leg on the way to the hospital.'
>
> 'Oh no, how?'
>
> 'She was hit by an ambulance on the way there.'

Explain why this is ironic.

Mrs Bennet, a character in *Pride and Prejudice* by Jane Austen, is a self-absorbed, overdramatic woman with no self-awareness and certainly no sense of humour. In the middle of a minor family crisis, she states:

> Nobody can tell what I suffer! But it is always so. Those who do not complain are never pitied.

1 Why is this statement ironic? Explain how this line fits the definition of irony.

Explore the skills

Read the first paragraph of this travel article by American humorist David Sedaris.

> I've never been much for guidebooks, so when trying to get my bearings in some strange American city, I normally start by asking the cabdriver or hotel clerk some silly question regarding the latest census figures. I say silly because I don't really care how many people live in Olympia, Washington or Columbus, Ohio. They're nice enough places, but the numbers mean nothing to me. My second question might have to do with the average annual rainfall, which, again, doesn't tell me anything about the people who have chosen to call this place home.
>
> David Sedaris, from 'Six to Eight Black Men'

2 What do you think of the tone of this travel article so far? Is it humorous, or simply informative?

Now read the second paragraph and the annotations.

> What really interests me are the local gun laws. Can I carry a concealed weapon and, if so, under what circumstances? What's the waiting period for a tommy gun? Could I buy a Glock 17 if I were recently divorced or fired from my job? I've learned from experience that it's best to lead into this subject as delicately as possible, especially if you and the local citizen are alone and enclosed in a relatively small area. Bide your time, though, and you can walk away with some excellent stories. I've learned, for example, that the blind can legally hunt in both Texas and Michigan. In Texas they must be accompanied by a sighted companion, but I heard that in Michigan they're allowed to go it alone, which raises the question: How do they find whatever it is they just shot? In addition to that, how do they get it home? Are the Michigan blind allowed to drive as well? I ask about guns not because I want one of my own but because the answers vary so widely from state to state. In a country that's become increasingly homogeneous, I'm reassured by these last charming touches of regionalism.

Annotations:
- a real shock after the first paragraph
- makes him sound obsessed with guns
- implying that he is aware that his questions sound sinister
- rhetorical questions paint quite an absurd picture
- an incongruous phrase to describe gun laws

Next, read the third paragraph, which develops the idea of learning about a new place.

> 'When do you open your Christmas presents?' is another good conversation starter, as I think it explains a lot about national character. People who traditionally open gifts on Christmas Eve seem a bit more pious and family-oriented than those who wait until Christmas morning. They go to Mass, open presents, eat a late meal, return to church the following morning, and devote the rest of the day to eating another big meal. Gifts are generally reserved for children, and the parents tend not to go overboard. It's nothing I'd want for myself, but I suppose it's fine for those who prefer food and family to things of real value.

Look at how one student has analysed the final sentence.

This sentence is ironic as Sedaris has described a traditional Christmas routine, with no trace of humour or irony. It is simply a descriptive account that most readers would recognise as a typical Christmas routine. The humour comes with the shock of his opinion: there is a gap between how we'd expect someone to react and how he actually reacts. Saying that 'food and family' are not of 'real value' is ironic because it suggests that Sedaris only values receiving gifts, which is funny because not only is he mocking himself, but also inviting the reader to examine their own attitude to Christmas.

3 Choose one annotation from the second paragraph and explain in a paragraph of your own why it is ironic. Use the student example above as a model.

4 Does Sedaris seem interested in learning about the places he visits? Write a paragraph explaining his overall viewpoint on travelling somewhere new.

> **Develop the skills**

In her travelogue *Travels In West Africa*, published in 1897, Mary Kingsley writes about her reactions to advice on a planned trip to West Africa.

I think many seemed to translate my request for practical hints and advice into an advertisement that 'Rubbish may be shot here.' This same information is in a state of great confusion still, although I have made heroic efforts to codify it. I find, however, that it can almost all be got in under the following different headings, namely and to wit:

- The dangers of West Africa
- The disagreeables of West Africa
- The diseases of West Africa
- The things you must take to West Africa
- The things you find most handy in West Africa
- The worst possible things you can do in West Africa.

[...]

It was the beginning of August '93 when I first left England for 'the Coast.' Preparations of **quinine** with postage partially paid arrived up to the last moment, and a friend hastily sent two newspaper clippings, one entitled 'A Week in a Palm-oil Tub,' which was supposed to describe the sort of accommodation, companions, and fauna likely to be met with on a steamer going to West Africa, and on which I was to spend seven to The Graphic contributor's one; the other from The Daily Telegraph, reviewing a French book of 'Phrases in common use' in **Dahomey**. The opening sentence in the latter was, 'Help, I am drowning.' Then came the inquiry, 'If a man is not a thief?' and then another cry, 'The boat is upset.' 'Get up, you lazy scamps,' is the next exclamation, followed almost immediately by the question, 'Why has not this man been buried?'

Mary Kingsley, from *Travels In West Africa*

Glossary

quinine: a treatment for malaria

Dahomey: a West African kingdom

5. What do Mary Kingsley's list of 'headings' suggest about the advice she has received? Is she being encouraged to travel to West Africa?

6. What do the gifts she receives suggest about her friends' attitude towards her journey?

7. What do the list of 'phrases in common use' suggest about how others feel about travelling to West Africa?

8. What do we learn about Kingsley's attitude towards travelling to West Africa? Does she seem put off by the advice she receives? Do you think she still travels there?

9. Overall, what is ironic about this extract?

Apply the skills

The ability to make clear connections between two texts is key to constructing a strong comparison.

The first step is to consider what the two texts have in common.

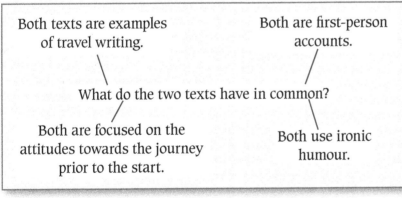

Both texts are examples of travel writing.

Both are first-person accounts.

What do the two texts have in common?

Both are focused on the attitudes towards the journey prior to the start.

Both use ironic humour.

10. Now use the following task to practise your comparison skills.

Compare the writers' views of travelling to a new place. Use evidence from both extracts to support your ideas.

Checklist for success

- Compare what we learn about both writers' views.
- Look at how the writers present these views to the reader.
- Explore the similarities and differences between the views.

Check your progress:

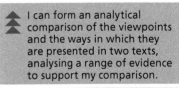

I can form an analytical comparison of the viewpoints and the ways in which they are presented in two texts, analysing a range of evidence to support my comparison.

I can present a detailed comparison between the viewpoints expressed in two texts, inferring meaning from a range of evidence.

I can make clear comparisons of viewpoint based on inferences from the text.

Compare the influence of poetic voices over time

Learning objectives

You will learn how to

- analyse and evaluate the ways poets from different centuries deal with a similar idea and perspective
- understand the idea of the sublime and how it relates to the Romantic movement.

Assessment objectives

- English Language AO3
- English Literature AO2

How can two writers see such different things in the same setting?

Getting you thinking

Romanticism was an important and influential artistic and cultural movement in the late eighteenth and early nineteenth centuries. One of the most important ideas in Romanticism is the sublime. The sublime deals with the powerful emotions and awe caused by the vastness, terror and beauty of nature. The sublime was concerned with the way the human mind responds to that awe by asserting its own creative and perceptive powers.

So, what does the sublime look like in literature? The following poem, 'Spellbound' by Emily Brontë, displays a conventional view of the sublime. The speaker of the poem is transfixed by the power of natural forces. This creates a powerful emotional response as she imagines the night to have captivated her.

Spellbound

The night is darkening round me,
The wild winds coldly blow;
But a tyrant spell has bound me
And I cannot, cannot go.

The giant trees are bending
Their bare boughs weighed with snow.
And the storm is fast descending,
And yet I cannot go.

Clouds beyond clouds above me,
Wastes beyond wastes below;
But nothing drear can move me;
I will not, cannot go.

Emily Brontë

1 **a** Brontë uses **personification** to bring the night and her surroundings to life. List as many examples as you can.

   b What effect do you think Brontë was trying to create by personifying the night?

   c How does the speaker feel about the natural world at this point in the poem?

   d How does she feel in comparison to the natural world?

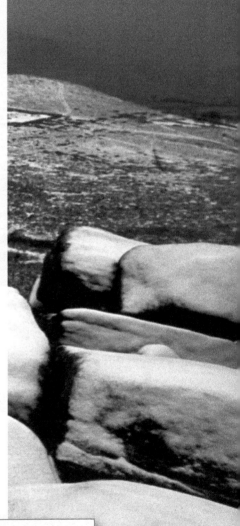

> **Key term**
>
> **personification:** a form of imagery where an inanimate object is given human characteristics

Explore the skills

Now read the following poem by Norman MacCaig published in 1969, over a hundred years after 'Spellbound'.

Below the Green Corrie

The mountains gathered round me
like bandits. Their leader
swaggered up close in the dark light,
full of threats, full of thunders.

But it was they who stood and delivered.
They gave me their money and their lives.
They filled me with mountains and thunders.

My life was enriched
with an infusion of theirs.
I clambered downhill through the ugly weather.
And when I turned to look goodbye
to those marvellous prowlers
a sunshaft had pierced the clouds
and their leader,
that swashbuckling mountain,
was wearing
a bandolier of light.

Norman MacCaig

2 MacCaig is also using personification to bring the natural world to life. List as many examples as you can.

Now look at two moments from the poems in close detail.

Spellbound

The night is darkening round me,
The wild winds coldly blow;
But a tyrant spell has bound me
And I cannot, cannot go.

Below the Green Corrie

The mountains gathered round me
like bandits. Their leader
swaggered up close in the dark light,
full of threats, full of thunders.

3 Look at the ideas collected in the following table. Find the evidence to support each detail. See how many more connections you can find between these two extracts from the poems.

Detail	Quotation	Effect
Both use repetition.		Both poets are suggesting the overwhelming presence of the natural world.
Both use an image of darkness.		Both seem to be suggesting that there is a dark, ominous presence about the natural world.
Both personify the natural world.		Both suggest that the natural world has a life-force which is dangerous and threatening.
Both suggest the idea of attack.		Both suggest the idea that nature is a threat to humans.

The main comparison to be made so far is that both poets have a similar view of nature. What is it?

4 Using the ideas from the table, write a summary of around 100 words of the ways nature and ideas about the natural world are presented in both poems. Find and include evidence to support your response.

Develop the skills

Both poets are clearly affected by the power of the natural world. MacCaig has used a very similar metaphor to Brontë, one of the key poets of the Romantic movement, to explore the idea of the relationship between humans and the natural world.

One of the main themes of Romantic literature was this relationship between people and nature. This theme has been explored by many writers since the time of the Romantic poets.

The American poet George Sterling explores the effect a mountain has on him in this poem, written in the very early twentieth century.

Night on the Mountain

The fog has risen from the sea and crowned
The dark, un-trodden summits of the coast,
Where roams a voice, in canyons uttermost,
From midnight waters vibrant and profound.
High on each granite altar dies the sound,
Deep as the trampling of an armored host,
Lone as the lamentation of a ghost,
Sad as the **diapason** of the drowned.

The mountain seems no more a soulless thing,
But rather as a shape of ancient fear,
In darkness and the winds of Chaos born
Amid the lordless heavens' thundering–
A Presence crouched, enormous and austere,
Before whose feet the mighty waters mourn.

George Sterling

> **Glossary**
> ....
>
> **diapason:** a full, beautiful, musical sound

5 Make a note of the words or phrases that suggest:
- darkness and misery
- fear and danger.

6 Now read the final stanza of 'Below the Green Corrie' again. As you read, compare how this speaker is affected by his experience.

7 Make a note of the words or phrases that suggest:
- a cheerful state of mind
- confidence.

Apply the skills

8 **Evaluate** 'Night on the Mountains' and 'Below the Green Corrie' against each other.

a What is the difference between the ways the poets are affected by their experience?

b What do these two extracts highlight?

Remember that the sublime:
- deals with powerful emotions such as fear and awe
- often explores ideas about the power, vastness and terror of the natural world
- deals with the beauty of nature and how its influence can be a positive force
- often refers to ideas about how a deep emotional connection with nature can unleash human genius and creative power.

9 Which of the two poems do you feel more closely expresses ideas about the sublime?

10 Thinking about the idea of the sublime, and how poets from two periods have interpreted it, complete the following task.

Compare the ways Sterling and MacCaig present ideas about the power of nature in 'Night on the Mountain' and 'Below the Green Corrie'.

Checklist for success
- Make clear comparisons between the ideas in both poems in order to evaluate the difference between the ways they are affected by their experience of the sublime.
- Use evidence to support your comments.
- Focus on how both writers have communicated their ideas.
- Comment on the similarities and the differences between the two viewpoints.

Key term

Evaluate: to judge the significance of something based on analysis of evidence

Check your progress:

I can present a comparative evaluation of the ways in which ideas about the sublime are communicated, making a judgment about which one is the more successful.

I can analyse the similarities and differences between the ways ideas about the sublime are presented in two poems, looking closely at the effects of a range of ways the writers have presented their ideas.

I can compare the ways ideas about the sublime are presented in two poems, using relevant evidence to support my ideas.

Compare and evaluate how writers explore similar ideas in poetry

Learning objective
You will learn how to
• construct an evaluative comparative response to two poems on a similar topic.

Assessment objective
• English Literature AO2

What is an 'evaluative comparison' and how do you do it?

'Evaluating' essentially means analysing evidence in order to make an informed judgment. Evaluating is like measuring; you are 'measuring the effectiveness' of something.

 Imagine you have been asked to evaluate the effectiveness of two vehicles. How would you start? Write a sentence explaining how you would go about evaluating the effectiveness of the two vehicles.

How did you reach your evaluation? It depends, doesn't it? It might depend on:

• whether you need to get somewhere quickly

• whether you need to carry lots of large heavy objects

• whether you need to impress somebody

• whether you need to get to your destination as cheaply as possible.

You can't 'evaluate the effectiveness' of something without knowing what you are evaluating it *against*. You need some criteria in order to make your judgement. Once you know what the vehicle is needed for, you can evaluate which one would be the most successful for that particular purpose.

Comparative evaluation is analysing two texts in order to make a judgement about which one achieves its purpose, or presents its idea, more successfully to the reader. Your considered judgement will be based on an analysis of evidence.

You are looking carefully and analytically at a text

Weighing the ideas and details against an idea, or a concept, or against a different text

Reaching a conclusion

Explore the skills

2 Read the following poem. As you read, consider what you learn about the experience of being a child in a war-torn area.

Children in Wartime

Sirens ripped open
the warm silk of sleep;
we ricocheted to the shelter
moated by streets
that ran with darkness.
People said it was a storm,
but flak
had not the right sound
for rain;
thunder left such huge craters
of silence,
we knew this was no giant
playing bowls.
And later,
when I saw the jaw of glass,
where once had hung
my window spun with stars;
it seemed the sky
lay broken on my floor.

Isobel Thrilling

Look at the first line in more detail. What does the language suggest about the experience of being a child in a war?

> Sirens **1** **2** ripped open **3**
> the warm silk **4** of sleep **5**

3 Select two more details from the poem and analyse them in the same way. Remember to focus on what the poet is suggesting about the experience of being a child in war.

4 **Synthesise** your ideas into one paragraph: what ideas is this poet presenting about childhood in war? Use evidence to support your analysis.

5 Now read the following poem by Vernon Scannell. As you read, note down what this poem has in common with 'Children in Wartime'.

1 the first word jolts the reader just like the child would be jolted from sleep

2 more than one siren; suggests really loud and enveloping

3 a harsh verb, suggesting violence and pain, as if the child's world is being torn or 'ripped' apart. Also personifying the sirens, increasing sense of threat

4 like a cocoon – as if the child is wrapped up and protected and the war has 'ripped' this apart. Also has connotations of parachute silk being 'ripped', which links to fear of invasion

5 alliteration suggests both the soothing sense of sleep and the scream of the sirens

Key term

Synthesise: to draw together, summarise

Incendiary

That one small boy with a face like pallid cheese
And burnt-out little eyes could make a blaze
As brazen, fierce and huge, as red and gold
And zany yellow as the one that spoiled
Three thousand **guineas** worth of property
And crops at Godwin's Farm on Saturday
Is frightening – as fact and metaphor:
An ordinary match intended for
The lighting of a pipe or kitchen fire
Misused may set a whole menagerie
Of flame-fanged tigers roaring hungrily.
And frightening, too, that one small boy should set
The sky on fire and choke the stars to heat
Such skinny limbs and such a little heart
Which would have been content with one warm kiss
Had there been anyone to offer this.

Vernon Scannell

Glossary

guineas: old coins, worth just over one pound

Look at the first two lines of this poem in more detail. What do we learn about the poet's attitude towards this child?

That one small **1** boy with a face like pallid **2** cheese
And burnt-out **3** little eyes **4**

1 implies powerless, young, innocent perhaps

2 pale, ill, weak

3 burnt-out suggests hopeless, powerless

4 links to the word 'small', reinforces how young and small he is

6 Select two more details from the poem and analyse them in the same way. Remember to focus on what you learn about the poet's attitude towards this child.

Develop the skills

So far you have looked at the poems in isolation. However, you will have noticed that there are many similarities between them, in particular the attitude towards childhood that both poets are presenting.

7 Read the following statements. Which one do you think you could say the most about and why?

Both poems portray a vivid picture of childhood.

Both poets view childhood as something to be cherished and protected.

Both poets suggest that breaking the innocence of childhood is tragic.

8 Using the statement you have selected, write a summary of the main similarities between the poems. You may wish to use the following sentence starter to help you:

Both of these poems present a similar attitude towards childhood...

There are some differences between the ways the two poets present their ideas. Look at how a student has commented on one of the main differences.

> In 'Children in Wartime', the title shows that the poet is focusing on all children rather than just one. She uses the second person plural, 'we ricocheted to the shelter' and 'we knew it was no giant'. The effect of this is that she is talking about all children, making it seem more universal than just personal. In 'Incendiary', Scannell does the opposite. He focuses on just one child all the way through. He introduces the poem with 'one small boy' and then repeats this phrase later in the poem, as if to remind the reader that we are just looking at one child in particular.

9 What other ideas could be included in this response? Explore how and why:

- Scannell might want to focus on just one child rather than lots of children and whether this one child represents children in general
- Thrilling changes her focus from 'we' to 'I' later in the poem and what the effect of this might be.

10 Using the ideas below and the sample response as a starting point, write a paragraph of your own about the ways in which both poets have referred to one or more child.

Another main difference between the two poems is the use of perspective. Thrilling uses first-person perspective while Scannell uses the third person.

11 What effect does the use of perspective have, do you think? Think about:

- who the poets seem to be 'speaking to'
- the message or idea they want to get across to the reader
- which one seems more reflective and why
- which one seems more angry and why.

Apply the skills

12 The following task will enable you to hone your comparative evaluation skills using the two poems studied earlier.

Compare the ways two poets present ideas about childhood innocence in 'Children in Wartime' and 'Incendiary'.

Checklist for success

- Hook your comparison onto one or two key ideas that are common to both poems.
- Analyse the similarities using evidence.
- Analyse the differences using evidence.
- Make a judgement about which poem you think is more successful in getting its message across and why.

Check your progress:

- I can present a comparative evaluation of the ways in which ideas about childhood innocence are communicated, making a judgement about which one is the more successful.

- I can analyse the similarities and differences between the ways ideas about childhood innocence are presented in two poems, looking closely at the effects of a range of ways the writers have presented their ideas.

- I can compare the ways ideas about childhood innocence are presented in two poems, using relevant evidence to support my ideas.

Apply your skills to English Language and English Literature tasks

Learning objectives
You will learn how to
- apply the key skills from this chapter to an English Language task
- apply the key skills from this chapter to an English Literature task
- reflect on your progress through looking at different responses to these tasks.

Assessment objectives
- English Language AO3
- English Literature AO2

Responding to an English Language task

1 Read Source 1, which is an editorial article from *The Guardian* about boxing, published in 2000. As you read it, make some notes on what you are learning about the writer's viewpoint on boxing.

Source 1

Few would doubt Muhammad Ali's place as one of the great figures of the last century. He achieved global fame as an athlete, became a powerful spokesman for his people and a principled advocate for social justice – even forfeiting his champion's title rather than serve in Vietnam. But perhaps his greatest achievement is not yet complete. The eloquent testimony of his own deterioration into disability may yet prove his lasting legacy. For Muhammad Ali, once boxing's shining exponent, is now a living warning of the dangers of the ring. He has been reduced to virtual immobility, his once-fast tongue slowed and slurred – all because he took punches for three decades.

We mention him now because of the fate of a less-starred fellow boxer. On Saturday night Paul Ingle sustained serious brain injuries after losing to South Africa's Mbulelo Botile in Sheffield. He spent yesterday in hospital, in a 'critical but stable' condition after surgeons laboured for two and half hours to remove a blood clot from his brain. Predictably, the British Boxing Board of Control has put on its concerned face, promising 'to launch an inquiry' and look for 'lessons to be learned'.

But these cliches are no longer good enough. Boxing cannot sincerely 'inquire' into the circumstances of Saturday's fight or look for lessons, as if what happened to Paul Ingle was a freak accident - like a plane collision or a rail crash. When a disaster of that kind strikes, it is because something wholly unexpected has happened. But for a man to suffer brain damage after his brain has been pummelled – deliberately and with precision – is wholly to be expected. It is no surprise at all. Ask Michael Watson, still confined to a wheelchair after his fight against Chris Eubank in 1991. Ask Gerald McClellan, beaten into a coma in 1995 and now in need of 24-hour-a-day care. Ask the family of Bradley Stone, killed by his 1994 bantamweight bout. Or take one last look at Muhammad Ali.

No liberal calls for a ban on any activity lightly. But we repeat our long-held belief that boxing has no place in a civilised society. To those who say a ban would only drive the sport underground, we point to bear-baiting and cock-fighting: they were banned and have all but vanished from British life. We wish the same fate for the sport which has laid waste to too many young men, including the greatest among them.

Leader, 'Ban this barbaric sport', from *The Guardian*, 18 December 2000

2 Now read Source 2, which is an essay on boxing by William Hazlitt written in 1822. Again, as you read, think about what you are learning about this writer's viewpoint on boxing.

Source 2

In the first round every one thought it was all over. After making play a short time, the Gas-man flew at his adversary like a tiger, struck five blows in as many seconds, three first, and then following him as he staggered back, two more, right and left, and down he fell, a mighty ruin. There was a shout, and I said, 'There is no standing this.' Neate seemed like a lifeless lump of flesh and bone, round which the Gas-man's blows played with the rapidity of electricity or lighting, and you imagined he would only be lifted up to be knocked down again. [...]

If there had been a minute or more allowed between each round, it would have been intelligible how they should by degrees recover strength and resolution; but to see two men smashed to the ground, smeared with gore, stunned, senseless, the breath beaten out of their bodies; and then, before you recover from the shock, to see them rise up with new strength and courage, stand steady to inflict or receive mortal offence, and rush upon each other, 'like two clouds over the Caspian' – this is the most astonishing thing of all: - this is the high and heroic state of man! [...] Ye who despise the FANCY, do something to show as much pluck, or as much self-possession as this, before you assume a superiority which you have never given a single proof of by any one action in the whole course of your lives! – When the Gas-man came to himself, the first words he uttered were, 'Where am I? What is the matter!' 'Nothing is the matter, Tom – you have lost the battle, but you are the bravest man alive.'

William Hazlitt, from 'The Fight'

3 Now look at this practice task and consider how you would respond to it.

Both sources are about attitudes towards boxing. Compare the writers' different viewpoints on boxing.

Checklist for success

A successful response should:

* demonstrate your understanding of both sources
* use quotations from the sources to support your answer
* compare the writers' viewpoints by looking at the similarities and the differences.

Reflecting on your progress

 Read the following response to this task. As you read, think about what the student has done well and what advice they might need in order to make more progress.

Response 1

Both of these writers have strong opinions on boxing. The writer of Source 1 argues very strongly that boxing should be banned. They use the example of what has happened to Muhammed Ali and how he is 'a living warning of the dangers of the ring'. Although the viewpoint seems at the start to be praising boxers, describing Ali as 'one of the great figures of the last century', it quickly moves into criticising boxing very strongly.

— clear understanding of viewpoint

— relevant, well-used supporting evidence

Source 2 does something similar. At the start the writer makes the description of the boxing match seem really violent and horrible with phrases like 'lifeless lump of flesh and bone' and 'two men smashed to the ground, smeared with gore, stunned, senseless, the breath beaten out of their bodies', using descriptive language and alliteration to paint a very vivid picture of the dramatic scene to the reader. However, it also describes them having 'strength and courage' and that one of them is 'the bravest man alive'. This suggests that the writer is admiring them and sees them as being brave and fearless.

— identifies a comparison of the way viewpoint is presented

— evidence used very skilfully with the inclusion of some subject terminology

— understanding of viewpoint in second source

The writers have very different viewpoints on boxing. Source 1 is arguing that boxing should be banned, whereas Source 2 is a description of a boxing match made to sound as if the writer thinks it is very exciting and that he admires the courage of the two boxers. Source 1 focuses on boxing in general with lots of statistics and facts to support the argument, whereas Source 2 is a very personal, descriptive account of attending a boxing match by someone who thought the experience was exciting and really admires the boxers.

— very clear explanation of the key difference in viewpoint

Comments on Response 1

This is a clear comparative response. Although the student has dealt with the sources separately, the final paragraph compares them very well, showing clear understanding of the difference in viewpoint. Evidence is used very well to support the points being made. There is some use of subject terminology to identify some of the language techniques being used, however, this could be more developed as it is commenting rather than analysing.

5 How could this sample response be improved? Using the middle rung of the Check your progress ladder at the end of this chapter, think about what advice you might give to this student in order to improve their work.

6 Now read Response 2. As you read, think about what the student has done that is an improvement on Response 1, and what advice this student might need in order to make even more progress.

Response 2

The fundamental difference between these sources is the perspective. Source 1 is arguing about boxing in general, using factual material to support the argument; four tragic stories are recounted in addition to the well-known story of Muhammed Ali. Source 2, on the other hand, gives a personal descriptive account of attending a match and the respect and admiration he has for the strength and determination of the two fighters.

— *very strong focus on main point of difference*

Source 1 argues strongly that the sport should be banned. The writer claims that surgeons 'laboured for two and a half hours' to save Paul Ingle who was hurt during a match. There is a suggestion here that the writer is very critical of a sport that causes so much effort to try to save someone's life when they have deliberately gone into the ring and 'been pummelled – deliberately with precision'. This writer clearly sees the sport and the damage it causes to be completely unnecessary and brutal

— *perceptive inference into effect of quotation*

– totally unlike the writer of Source 2, who describes the violence as something honourable: 'flew at his adversary like a tiger' and 'high and heroic state of man'. This writer has chosen to attend a match and is very excited and uplifted by what he describes as the 'strength and courage' of the fighters. His viewpoint is completely different – rather than condemning the waste and brutality of the sport, he sees it as uplifting and admirable: 'you are the bravest man alive'.

— *use of well-chosen evidence to support a strong comparison*

— *another strong comparative comment*

Comments on Response 2

This response identifies a very strong difference between the texts and builds their answer from this key difference. The comparison runs through the whole of the response, with some very good inferences made, well supported with some precise evidence.

Responding to an English Literature task

1 Read the following poem, written in 1918. As you read, think about these questions:

- What is this poem about?
- What ideas and feelings do you think the writer is communicating?
- What do you notice about the ways language, structure and form have been used to communicate these ideas and feelings to the reader?

Piano

Softly, in the dusk, a woman is singing to me;
Taking me back down the vista of years, till I see
A child sitting under the piano, in the boom of the tingling strings
And pressing the small, poised feet of a mother who smiles as she sings.

In spite of myself, the insidious mastery of song
Betrays me back, till the heart of me weeps to belong
To the old Sunday evenings at home, with winter outside
And hymns in the cosy parlour, the tinkling piano our guide.

So now it is vain for the singer to burst into clamour
With the great black piano appassionato. The glamour
Of childish days is upon me, my manhood is cast
Down in the flood of remembrance, I weep like a child for the past.

D.H. Lawrence

2 Now read the following poem, written in 1984. As you read, remember to think about:

- What is this poem about?
- What ideas and feelings do you think the writer is communicating?
- What do you notice about the ways language, structure and form have been used to communicate these ideas and feelings to the reader?

Background Material

My writing desk. Two photos, mam and dad.
A birthday, him. Their ruby wedding, her.
Neither one a couple and both bad.
I make out what's behind them from the blur.

Dad's in our favourite pub, now gone for good.
My father and his background are both gone,
but hers has my Welsh cottage and a wood
that still shows those same greens eight summers on,
though only the greenness of it's stayed the same.

Though one of them's in colour and one's not,
the two are joined, apart from their shared frame,
by what, for photographers, would mar each shot:

in his, if you look close, the gleam, the light,
me in his blind right eye, but minute size –

in hers, as though just cast from where I write,
a shadow holding something to its eyes.

Tony Harrison

3 Now look at this practice task and consider how you would respond to it.

Compare the ways poets present attitudes towards the past in 'Piano' and 'Background Material'.

Checklist for success

A successful response should:

- compare the poems, looking at the links and connections between them
- demonstrate your understanding of ideas and feelings in both poems
- include some well-selected evidence to support your comparison
- analyse the effects of particular words, literary techniques, structural features and aspects of the form of both poems, linked to the ideas and feelings in both poems
- evaluate the ways both poems present attitudes towards the past.

Reflecting on your progress

4 Read the following section of a response to this task. As you read, think about what the student has done well and what advice they might need in order to make more progress.

Response 1

Both 'Piano' and 'Background Material' are about the speaker's feelings of love towards their parents. Both are looking back to the past, and both use one specific event to be reminded of the past; hearing a piano playing in 'Piano', and looking at a pair of photographs in 'Background Material'. Both poets use language to create a specific, similar mood. Lawrence describes his mother having 'small, poised feet' and 'smiles as she sings', which uses specific details to suggest the idea that he felt lots of love and admiration for her. Harrison similarly shows his connection to his mother standing outside 'my Welsh cottage' by a wood that 'still shows those same greens' as if she is part of nature and alive.

— clear connection made, showing understanding of both poems

— simple statement

— good use of evidence to support comment on feelings

— clear connection between the way both poets feel about their mothers

Comments on Response 1

This is promising but the student has some work to do. They have established a clear connection between the two poems and shown very clear understanding of ideas and feelings. They know how to use supporting evidence. However, some of the comments need to be more developed.

5 How could this sample response be improved? Using the middle rung of the Check your progress ladder at the end of this chapter, think about what advice you might give to this student in order to improve their work.

6 Now read the paragraph below where the student has taken one part of their answer and improved it. As you read, think about what the student has done that is an improvement.

Response 2

> Both poets use language to create a specific mood. In 'Piano', Lawrence describes a memory of being underneath the piano, as if he is enclosed and dark, or protected from the outside world by being close to his mother. This idea is reinforced with the repetition of 'weep' and the 'black' of the piano. His feelings are 'betray[ing]' him, showing his yearning to be protected from the outside world by the 'Sunday evenings at home, with winter outside'. In contrast, Harrison associates his mother with nature, spring and growth; her photo is contrasted with that of his father with a semantic field of colour, reinforced by 'ruby / green / greens / colour', as if the memory of his mother is linked to life and vibrancy. Perhaps what the reader draws from this is that Lawrence is mourning the protection offered by his mother, whereas Harrison is celebrating the energy of his connection to his parents, in particular his mother, and how 'the gleam, the light', reminds him of how they are still connected to each other.

developed comment on language effects with some relevant examples

beginning to interpret feelings, using evidence to make some skilful inferences

lovely comparison between the effects of language in both poems

an evaluative comparison of the feelings in both poems

Check your progress

- I can form an evaluative comparison of the viewpoints and ideas in two texts, and the ways in which they are presented.
- I can closely analyse precise selections of evidence to support my analytical comparison.
- I can evaluate the ways in which ideas are communicated, making a judgement about which one is the more successful.

- I can form an analytical comparison between the viewpoints expressed in two texts.
- I can analyse a range of evidence from both texts to support my analytical comparison.
- I can analyse the similarities and differences between the ways ideas are presented in two texts, looking closely at the effects of a range of ways the writers have presented their ideas.

- I can present a detailed comparison between the viewpoints expressed in two texts.
- I can select and use details from both texts to present a detailed comparison of viewpoint.
- I can begin to analyse the similarities and differences between the ways a similar idea or topic is presented in two texts.

Chapter 8

Writing creatively

What's it all about?

In this chapter, you will explore the techniques that make the very best creative writing, in the form of narratives or descriptions, come alive. You will look at how writers create convincing, compelling voices that draw us into their world. You will explore the ways in which writers address powerful ideas about the way we live, or our place in the world. You will also see how writers experiment with conventional techniques and styles of writing to give the reader unusual and surprising perspectives.

In this chapter, you will learn how to

- engage the reader through original forms of narration
- use imagery and symbolism to enhance narrative and descriptive power
- use structures to create memorable texts
- apply your skills to an English Language task.

	English Language GCSE	
Which AOs are covered?	AO5 Communicate clearly, effectively and imaginatively, selecting and adapting tone, style and register for different forms, purposes and audiences Organise information and ideas, using structural and grammatical features to support coherence and cohesion of texts	AO6 Candidates must use a range of vocabulary and sentence structures for clarity, purpose and effect, with accurate spelling and punctuation
How will this be tested?	Questions will require you to apply what you have learned about the overall organisation of texts so that they are consciously crafted to create effects on readers. They will also require you to write for one of two purposes – to describe or to narrate – so you will need to show your ability to adapt, manipulate and craft language appropriately.	Questions will require you to think of original, compelling ways of expressing yourself through your choice of vocabulary and sentences. You will be expected to demonstrate a rich and ambitious vocabulary.

Engage the reader through original forms of narration

How can you engage the reader through narrative forms or voices?

Getting you thinking

This is the opening to a story called 'Wreckage'.

> Of course being young, shiny and vibrant I did not expect to die so young. But then Spring is soon past, and Autumn soon upon us. For me the Spring was birth in a factory on the other side of the world; Autumn was a bend on the motorway when Suki lost control and I ended up on my side on a barren highway, wondering why there were flames belching from my body and Suki staring at me from the side of the road, shaking uncontrollably in the stutter of the police lights. But through the tears, I saw it in her eyes: I was finished.

1 Who is narrating this extract?

2 What do we learn about the narrator and their relationships?

3 In what way is the writer trying to engage the reader in the opening sentence of the story?

Explore the skills

Choosing an unusual narrative voice for a text can be one way of making what could be a dull tale come alive. For example, you could:

- give something inanimate or not human a voice
- make the narrator a 'phantom' or double of the main character in some way (for example, a voice from the dead or a younger self)
- make the narrator an observer or someone who does not appear to be central to the story
- place the narrator in an unusual situation or position from which 'normal' description is difficult
- use a combination of these ideas!

4 Which of the narrative perspectives above can you link to the following short extracts? Jot down:

- who the narrator is
- what they are seeing or describing
- what makes them engaging or interesting as narrators.

a I'm not quite clear why things have changed between us. All I know is that my bowl isn't filled as regularly as it once was, and I'm as likely to get a slap as a pat on the back…

b For a moment, he wished he could rise out of his body, still and flat on the hospital bed and look down on the family as they inspected him. Of course, all he actually saw was the upper half of his father's face, a sweaty brow, and grey eyes peering, like marbles, through the porthole of his world.

c They met at my stall. That first day, she dropped her change and he picked it up. She smiled, they laughed nervously, and he pressed the fifty pence piece into her hands. They left in separate directions, but the next day they were here at the same time, chatting, exchanging looks. I was invisible.

d She doesn't know it yet, but one day she will be me. Now, she is a seven year old, proud of her brittle sandcastle, neither she, nor it, fully formed. I watch her, a phantom of the future, helpless to alter her choices, the cold tide coming in. Of course, you are there, too, observing her from the rocks at a distance, her best friend forever…or so she thinks.

5 Each of the above narratives suggests something about a relationship (or relationships). Write down:

- what the relationship is
- any clues given about its history or its future development.

Develop the skills

Choosing who your narrator is and selecting someone more unusual or in an unusual situation can make your writing more original, but just as important is the tone, the voice you adopt. Read this opening to the novel *High Fidelity* by Nick Hornby.

> My desert-island, all time, top five most memorable split-ups, in chronological order:
> 1) Alison Ashworth
> 2) Penny Hardwick
> 3) Jackie Allen
> 4) Charlie Nicholson
> 5) Sarah Kendrew
>
> These were the ones that really hurt. Can you see your name in that lot Laura? I reckon you'd sneak into the top ten, but there's no place for you in the top five; those places are reserved for the kind of humiliations and heartbreaks that you're just not capable of delivering. This probably sounds crueller than it is meant to, but the fact is that we're too old to make each other miserable, and that's a good thing, not a bad thing, so don't take your failure to make the list personally.
>
> Nick Hornby, from *High Fidelity*

6 Who is the narrator addressing here? (This may be more than one person.)

7 Should we trust what he says about Laura? Why / why not?

8 What does the use of a 'desert-island' style list to categorise former girlfriends suggest about the narrator? How might this be linked to the title of the novel?

9 What language features can we see here that contribute to the distinctive voice and style? See if you can find examples of any elements below.

Informal, chatty vocabulary and turns of phrase	Semicolons used to add a clarification to the previous statement
Vivid, descriptive setting	Third-person narrator
Directly addressing another character	Past tense references to past events
First-person narrator	Present tense references to current situations
Reflective thoughts on emotions	Exclamation marks for shock or anger

Key term

tone: suggests an attitude in the 'voice' that is 'speaking' to you in the text, for example, through the words used, the way sentences are phrased and the level of formality

10 What overall **tone** is created?

11 Now look again at the four extracts (a, b, c, d) in Activity 4.

   a What tone of voice is used in each case?

   b What language clues indicate this?

For example, how do the following uses of metaphor **1** and the short end clause **2** create a particular tone in the fourth example? What is the tone?

> I watch her, a phantom of the future, helpless to alter her choices, the cold tide coming in.**1** Of course, you are there, too, observing her from the rocks at a distance, her best friend forever… or so she thinks.**2**

12 Choose one of the short extracts from Activity 4 and continue it, maintaining a similar style and narrative perspective.

Apply the skills

Read this task.

> Write a description or story suggested either by the photo or the title 'Long Division'.

13 Consider the following approach before tackling the task above.

- Begin by generating some ideas around the title and/or photo, in order to come up with suggestions about the situation or relationship. Try to think beyond the obvious: relationships can be between all sorts of people (family members, friends, leaders and followers, and so on).

- Decide on a narrator. Go back to the possibilities you have encountered in this unit, and think about what would make an interesting or original perspective. If you are using the picture, it could be someone out of shot, not necessarily the people shown. Or you could alternate between two different narrators, with different narrative voices.

- Plan the style of narrative voice and how you will create it.

Check your progress:

▲▲ I can create a range of convincing, original and compelling narrative voices and perspectives which engage the reader from the first sentence of the story.

▲ I can create some engaging and convincing narrative voices and perspectives.

▲ I can create different narrative voices and perspectives.

Checklist for success

- Make your narrator interesting and engaging.
- Match the language and style to the story told, or the relationships revealed.

Use imagery and symbolism to enhance narrative and descriptive power

Learning objectives
You will learn how to
- use imagery and symbolism to add power to your stories
- draw on wider ideas to create interesting connections for the reader.

Assessment objectives
- English Language AO5, AO6

How can you make your stories and descriptions distinctive and powerful?

Getting you thinking

Read this short **cinquain**.

The Warning

Just now,
Out of the strange
Still dusk – as strange, as still –
A white moth flew. Why am I grown
So cold?

Adelaide Crapsey

1 On the surface, the **literal** meaning is simply that of a moth appearing as night falls. But is that all the poet wants to convey? Write brief answers to these questions.

   a What might the 'white moth' represent?

   b Why do you think the poet chose a moth, rather than a butterfly?

Explore the skills

Use of powerful **imagery** such as the 'white moth' appearing out of the strange twilight can convey or **symbolise** lots of ideas. These are created by the connotations that come to mind from the image – whether this is frailty, destruction or something else.

2 Weather and the seasons are typically used to symbolise emotions or life's progress. Complete one of the cinquains below, or write your own, trying to convey a deeper or more powerful idea.

a Here lies	b Dark clouds	c Our house
The fallen tree …	Gather by us …	Glows with bright sun …

Now read the opening to this short story by Ted Hughes, 'The Rain Horse'. In the story, a man comes back to the countryside area he left twelve years earlier.

> As the young man came over the hill the first thin blowing of rain met him. He turned his coat-collar up and stood on top of the shelving rabbit-riddled hedgebank, looking down into the valley. He had come too far. What had set out as a walk along pleasantly-remembered tarmac lanes had turned dreamily by gate and path into a cross-ploughland trek, his shoes ruined, the dark mud of the lower fields inching up the trouser legs of his grey suit where they rubbed against each other. And now there was a raw, flapping wetness in the air that would be downpour at any minute. He shivered, holding himself tense against the cold.
>
> Ted Hughes, from 'The Rain Horse'

Annotations:
- the weather begins to change
- suggests he has lost his way
- the happy memories, almost dream-like, are replaced by reality
- wearing business clothes

3 On the surface, all this story seems to be about is a man who has got lost in the countryside. But is there more to it than that? Look at the annotations, and then make notes on:

a the narrator's situation and the error he has made

b how conditions have changed

c any phrases or sentences that suggest there is more to this than just a ruined walk.

4 Think about the young man returning after twelve years. What could this extract suggest about his decision to return?

Now read this later extract from the same story.

> Twelve years had changed him. This land no longer recognized him, and he looked back at it coldly, as at a finally visited home country, known only through the stories of a grandfather…

Key terms

figurative language: words or phrases that represent or symbolise other ideas, not just literal ones

personification: a type of metaphor where something inanimate or inhuman is given human characteristics

5 Hughes uses **figurative language** in two further ways here. Identify:

a his use of **personification** in how the countryside responds *to him*

b his use of comparison in how he responds *to the countryside*.

6 How do these descriptions build on the earlier idea of him being unwelcome or out of place?

7 Copy and complete the following statements to create similar personifications:

   a The countryside turned its... on him.

   b The sky covered its... and disappeared.

   c The mouth of the valley... .

8 Now choose one set of features of the landscape he is in from the following list:

   - mud, earth, soil
   - trees, shrubs, woods
   - fences, hedges, gates
   - hills, slopes, mounds.

   Write a paragraph which presents your chosen aspect as unwelcoming to the character. You could use these techniques to help you:

   - personification in the form of verbs related to conflict ('attacked', 'battered')

   - negative adjectives or nouns ('foreign', 'stranger')

   - unpleasant similes to describe key features ('hawthorn hedges *like barbed wire*').

Develop the skills

The central idea of the landscape being unwelcoming is taken a stage further in the story when a black horse suddenly charges at him, and he is forced to hide. Just as he is beginning to think the attack is a one-off, it happens again.

> The black shape was above him, right across the light. Its whinnying snort and the spattering whack of its hooves seemed to be actually inside his head as he fell backwards down the bank, and leapt again like a madman dodging among the oaks, imagining how the buffet would come and how he would be knocked headlong. Halfway down the wood the oaks gave way to bracken and old roots and stony rabbit diggings. He was well out into the middle of this before he realized he was running alone.

horse creates darkness

so powerful it seems to be in his mind

Gasping for breath now and cursing mechanically, without a thought for his suit he sat down on the ground to rest his shaking legs, letting the rain plaster his hair down over his forehead and watching the dense flashing lines disappear abruptly into the soil all around him as if he were watching through thick plate glass. He took deep breaths in the effort to steady his heart and regain control of himself. His right trouser turn-up was ripped at the seam and his suit jacket was splashed with the yellow mud of the top field.

now more focused on survival than how he looks

 9 The power of the narrative comes from the details of the horse's actions and of the man's reactions and feelings. Through these, Hughes begins to suggest or imply other ideas.

Looking over the annotations, make brief notes about:
- the idea that the horse may symbolise something more than just a vicious or startled animal
- how his own behaviour and priorities have now changed
- whether Hughes is making wider points about man and nature.

Apply the skills

10 Read this task.

Write the opening to a story in which someone gets lost in an unfamiliar environment.

Use the following steps to guide you through completing the task.

a Briefly, jot down some ideas for your story:
- *Who* is lost? Will there be *anyone else* (or thing) in the story?
- *Where* are they lost/*Where* have they come from?
- *How* did it happen?

b Now, think about how you can represent the relationship between the setting and the person who is lost. It does not need to be alien or unwelcoming, but could be a refreshing change or new experience.

c Draft your opening three paragraphs. You could begin with the familiar and then move onto the unfamiliar, increasing the emotional and physical effects.

Checklist for success
- Suggest a deeper meaning to the story than simply a tale of someone getting lost through imagery or symbolism.
- Use personification to describe inanimate or natural objects.
- Choose verbs and nouns carefully to imply the relationship between place and person.

Check your progress:

 I can sustain a powerful range of ideas through my selection of imagery and symbols.

 I can use appropriate imagery and symbolism in my writing to create vivid narratives.

 I can use some imagery to make my writing more vivid.

Use structures to create memorable texts

Learning objectives

You will learn how to
- use structure to produce an interesting and coherent narrative
- develop themes or ideas to suggest moods and tones in a story
- use shape and structure of the whole text to give an overall 'completeness'.

Assessment objectives
- English Language AO5, AO6

How can you order and structure narratives to interest and engage the reader?

Getting you thinking

At the heart of all writing is structure, and in narratives that means the particular arrangement of events, and the way and the order in which the writer reveals the story to us.

Read this opening line to a short story called 'Miss Brill' by Katherine Mansfield.

> Although it was so brilliantly fine—the blue sky powdered with gold and great spots of light like white wine splashed over the *Jardins Publiques*—Miss Brill was glad that she had decided on her fur.
>
> Katherine Mansfield, from 'Miss Brill'

Glossary

Jardins Publiques: public park/gardens

1. Who are we introduced to in this opening line?
2. What is happening?
3. Is there any other way this sentence could have been arranged?
4. Can you think of any reason why the writer ordered it like this?

Explore the skills

A key part of the structure is the opening. It can do many things:
- set the scene (tell us where and when things are happening)
- introduce minor or key characters
- suggest themes or ideas that might prove to be important later
- establish a tone or mood
- show a particular event or action taking place which may have later significance.

In the opening line, the writer begins with a subordinate clause which starts with a word ('Although') indicating qualification or even negativity: even though it was nice weather, the main character feels cold, so wears fur. This suggests (and it is only a hint) that this may not turn out to be a perfectly happy tale.

Other structural features relate to the time order of events. Now read the whole opening paragraph to 'Miss Brill'.

Although it was so brilliantly fine—the blue sky powdered with gold and great spots of light like white wine splashed over the *Jardins Publiques*—Miss Brill was glad that she had decided on her fur. The air was motionless, but when you opened your mouth there was just a faint chill, like a chill from a glass of iced water before you sip, and now and again a leaf came drifting—from nowhere, from the sky. Miss Brill put up her hand and touched her fur. Dear little thing! It was nice to feel it again. She had taken it out of its box that afternoon, shaken out the moth-powder, given it a good brush, and rubbed the life back into the dim little eyes. "What has been happening to me?" said the sad little eyes. Oh, how sweet it was to see them snap at her again from the red eiderdown!…But the nose, which was of some black composition, wasn't at all firm. It must have had a knock, somehow. Never mind—a little dab of black sealing-wax when the time came—when it was absolutely necessary…Little rogue! Yes, she really felt like that about it. Little rogue biting its tail just by her left ear. She could have taken it off and laid it on her lap and stroked it. She felt a tingling in her hands and arms, but that came from walking, she supposed. And when she breathed, something light and sad—no, not sad, exactly—something gentle seemed to move in her bosom.

opening establishes the current situation

signals earlier action

returns us to the present moment

Short stories require economy, conveying a great deal in not many sentences. They often focus on one current or ongoing moment, rather than plodding through everything that has happened in strict time order.

5   The story begins in the public gardens, but what *earlier* event are we then told about?

6   What verb form ('had taken', 'has taken' or 'took') does the writer use to indicate this event that has been completed?

7   What do we learn about how Miss Brill feels about the fox fur *now*?

8   What verb form ('bitten', 'bite', 'biting', 'had bitten') tells us this is what she is experiencing at this moment in the story?

9   In Mansfield's story, there is also a young couple in the
gardens. Write a similar first few lines about them as they,
too, arrive at the park.

Start with a sentence about them and
what they are doing as they arrive in
the park. For example…

> Luke and Estelle pushed open the gate and ran
> into the open space, scattering the pigeons…

Then, go back in time to reveal earlier
events or actions between them (use
the past perfect 'had' form).

> Just an hour ago, they…

Finally, write a sentence establishing
something happening to them now
(use the participle '…ing' form).

> Here, …ing in the park…

Develop the skills

The structuring of a narrative or description is also made memorable
by echoes and patterns that imply ideas or moods and tones. We
have already seen how the story opens with a qualifying conjunction
that hints at all not being well.

10   Where in the text does Mansfield use 'but' to:

- emphasise the coldness in the air
- indicate the fox fur isn't completely restored?

11   What other descriptions hint at or add to this sense of things
being not quite perfect, or at a darker side to the story?

12   Copy and complete these sentences about the same young
couple in the park; add suitable conjunctions to hint at not
everything being well. Choose from: *but, even though,
although, yet.*

> [Conjunction] *the water in the duck lake looked
> clear and blue at a distance, there was…*

> *They had hoped to find a
> quiet spot to sit and chat,*
> [conjunction] *a…*

> *The boy hugged the girl close
> to him,* [conjunction] *she…*

Now read the ending of 'Miss Brill'. She is watching a band play on the bandstand and a young couple come and sit near her, the boy trying to kiss the girl.

"No, not now," said the girl. "Not here, I can't."

"But why? Because of that stupid old thing at the end there?" asked the boy. "Why does she come here at all—who wants her? Why doesn't she keep her silly old mug at home?"

"It's her fu-ur which is so funny," giggled the girl. "It's exactly like a fried whiting."

"Ah, be off with you!" said the boy in an angry whisper. Then: "Tell me, ma petite chère—"

"No, not here," said the girl. "Not yet."

On her way home she usually bought a slice of honey-cake at the baker's. It was her Sunday treat. Sometimes there was an almond in her slice, sometimes not. It made a great difference. If there was an almond it was like carrying home a tiny present—a surprise—something that might very well not have been there. She hurried on the almond Sundays and struck the match for the kettle in quite a dashing way.

But today she passed the baker's by, climbed the stairs, went into the little dark room—her room like a cupboard—and sat down on the red eiderdown. She sat there for a long time. The box that the fur came out of was on the bed. She unclasped the necklet quickly; quickly, without looking, laid it inside. But when she put the lid on she thought she heard something crying.

The way in which the ending echoes or draws upon earlier ideas can give the structure of a short story a sense of overall 'completeness'.

13 In what ways does the ending:

- develop the earlier theme of spinsterhood
- link back to earlier events or things Miss Brill has done?

Apply the skills

14 Before embarking on the task below, draft a plan with main character(s), setting and the basic elements of the plot.

Write your own story called 'The Anniversary'.

Checklist for success

- Reveal past and present information fluently by your use of tenses.
- Hint or indicate mood or tone through your use of conjunctions or sentence order.
- Create a 'completeness' in your story by echoing or coming back to earlier events or themes in your final paragraph.

Check your progress:

- I can use structural devices fluently and inventively to create a range of ideas and effects.
- I can use structural devices to make my writing coherent and engaging.
- I can link ideas effectively using some structural devices.

Apply your skills to an English Language task

Learning objectives
You will learn how to
- apply the key skills from this chapter to an English Language task
- reflect on your progress through looking at different responses to the task.

Assessment objectives
- English Language AO5, AO6

Responding to an English Language task

1 Consider the following task and how you would respond to it.

Your task
You are going to enter a creative writing competition. In the competition you have to write a description suggested by the photo below.

Think about:
- what you can see in this picture
- how you could create a vivid and detailed description for the reader.

Checklist for success

A successful response should include:

- a convincing, original and compelling narrative voice to engage the reader

- vivid details and imagery to reflect the natural world and the synthetic things in the picture

- a structure that creates and links a range of ideas and effects inspired by the image.

Reflecting on your progress

 2 Read the following response to this task. As you read, think about what the student has done well and what advice they might need in order to make more progress.

Response 1

Under the sea the only sound at first is the air pressure against your scuba mask. The world is silent and dark and you struggle to make out shapes. Then, slowly, it all comes into focus and you make sense of the world around you. The huge ship is tilted on its side and is a monster, but one that is asleep. It seems to be groaning but it is all in the mind. Everything remains still and it feels as if you're the only thing in deep sea universe.

— narrative voice implied by use of 'you' and 'your'

— metaphors personify the ship

The round port-holes in the side of the ship are eyes staring out into the blackness. If you shine a torch deep into the sockets you will see there is no life there at all. If you run your hands along the rusty edge that feels so rough and hard, you will feel the metal like jagged jaws that could cut like daggers. And if you run your hand along the top you will feel the slime of centuries.

— rhetorical patterning of 'If you' is repeated

Inside the old ship's body you feel tense. What if there are bodies still here, even though it has been centuries since the ship sank? There are eyes watching you, or so you think, as you push open the creaky metal door into the lower bit. Groping for something to hold, you descend. Into the darkness as if into hell. Then at the bottom you turn and cast your torch light on the corridor. The glow goes around the walls lighting up rusty shelves. Your feet crunch on old, dirty cups on the floor, so you flip your flippers to break free and go along the space towards the cabins. This is a place you fear but you must face.

— effective short sentence sums up by referring back

— phrase echoes the opening of the text

Under your gaze, groups of little silver fish flash in front of your eyes and for a moment you forget your reason for being there. The water is green and grimy here too, and you're glad you can't taste it, just the oxygen you're breathing all the time.

So, you push open the first cabin door. But nothing happens. It is rusted fast onto its old warped hinges. Taking out a small axe from your belt, you bash away at the hinges until even through the mask you hear a welcome crack. Slowly the door opens inwards and you point your fading torch light at the cabin.

— focused detail

At first it is indistinct. Then the image grows and you see a white figure lying on the bed.

— pronoun 'it' is foregrounded, making the reader wait to find out more

Rags which were once clothes hang from the poor dead soul's tatty frame. It is a skeleton of someone drowned while dreaming – they never had a chance, and now they're here forever asleep. You reach down to pull the chain from around the corpse's neck. It won't come off so you wrench and pull till suddenly the whole head and neck fall off. You scream inside your mask and turn for the exit.

Under the spell of the dead ship, you do not know what else you will find, so you decide to head for the surface. Something has spooked you deep inside and you can't face going back. You take one last look at the rotting ship and swim upwards towards the light.

— phrase echoes opening of text

Comments on Response 1

This response is reasonably effective but occasionally strays into narrative when it could perhaps build and develop ideas, such as the symbolic notion of the ship as a monster or a dead creature. There are also several opportunities to allude or draw on other stories or myths, such as descent into the underworld, or notions of souls in limbo (the skeleton which will be always 'asleep' in the ship) or references to piracy on the high seas. There are some good attempts to try to create echoes or patterns of phrases, such as the repeated use of 'Under' but these could be more ambitious; this also means the voice of the narrator is rather bland and detached, when it should be more original and memorable.

3 How could this sample response be improved? Using the middle rung of the Check your progress ladder at the end of this chapter, think about what advice you might give to this student in order to improve their work.

4 Now read Response 2. As you read, think about what the student has done that is an improvement on Response 1, and what advice this student might need in order to make even more progress.

Response 2

Above, I am invisible.
I am a dead orchestra. I am a thousand sounds that cannot be heard in the chambers of the ocean. I am one, yet I am many. The notes from my music are airy bubbles that float into nothingness. My players are the gaping port-holes, wind instruments that belch out sonic booms into blue nothingness. My strings are the leaves of sea plants that wave and curl in the current and tide.

— powerful metaphor

— imagery is developed and extended across the paragraph

I sing a dead song. It is a song I repeat for infinity, a song of a hopeful journey turned into despair. It is a song of a captain who lost his way. For all humans lose their way on the journey of life, on the voyage of life, in the path through the forest of waves and calm. Up, down, up, down. Swinging high, low, high, low. Slowly, I will disappear into the ashes of the ocean floor, taking with me the memories and the history. My past in the dockyards of the north, my free adventures around the globe and my passing several centuries ago. I can feel my old body sinking into the arms of the ocean bed, a terrible destructive embrace.

I shall sing my song as I descend into the coffin of the earth. There are many of us who rest here in the graveyard of the ocean: tiny dinghies that capsized on pleasure trips; trawlers that took their fishermen with them; motorboats who disappeared during races. Dotted around the globe, we are an underwater army that no one sees.

Can you hear us? If you put your ear to a shell on a sandy beach you will hear a roar. This is not the sea but our souls crying out for rest.

Listen out for us as you pass on your own voyages. Do not forget us.

We are below you.

rhetorical patterning mimics the roll of the ocean

literal reference amongst the abstract and figurative

personification of ocean is vivid and original

effective use of colons and semicolons to embellish the idea

effective final line acts as summary and extension of what has just been described

alludes to childhood game

final short sentence is literally as well as figuratively 'below' and also links back to the first sentence

Comments on Response 2

This is a rich and evocative re-imagining, using the picture as a prompt. The compelling metaphors which draw parallels between life's journey and actual travel are original, and the overall structure and composition with its echoes and repetitions fits the idea of a sunken boat.

Occasionally, the metaphors and abstractions seem to contradict each other, and perhaps drift a little bit away from the source but in general, the range of vocabulary, the choice of imagery and the variety in sentences and overall arrangement create an ambitious and original piece.

Check your progress

- I can create a range of convincing, original and compelling narrative voices and perspectives which engage the reader from the first sentence of the story.

- I can sustain a powerful range of ideas through my selection of imagery and symbols.

- I can use structural devices fluently and inventively to create a range of ideas and effects.

- I can create engaging and effective narrative voices and perspectives.

- I can use appropriate imagery and symbolism in my writing to create vivid narratives.

- I can use structural devices to make my writing coherent and engaging.

- I can create a range of different narrative voices and perspectives.

- I can use imagery to make my writing more vivid.

- I can link ideas effectively using some structural devices.

Chapter 9
Point of view writing

What's it all about?

In this chapter, you will explore and apply the techniques that writers use to create a convincing and engaging point of view. You will explore how to build a convincing argument or voice around an idea using extended metaphors or other methods, vary the structure of your writing in inventive ways, and subtly alter or manipulate your tone and style to match purpose, form and audience.

In this chapter, you will learn how to

- convey convincing and original voices in your writing
- manipulate structure to create effects in point-of-view writing
- match style and tone to purpose and audience
- apply your skills to an English Language task.

	English Language GCSE	
Which AOs are covered?	AO5 Communicate clearly, effectively and imaginatively, selecting and adapting tone, style and register for different forms, purposes and audiences Organise information and ideas, using structural and grammatical features to support coherence and cohesion of texts	AO6 Candidates must use a range of vocabulary and sentence structures for clarity, purpose and effect, with accurate spelling and punctuation
How will this be tested?	Questions will require you to consider a range of possibilities to draw your reader in, for example, by altering or foregrounding particularly important ideas, and in how you link and move between the points you wish to make.	Questions will require you to express your opinion with consistently accurate, ambitious and wide-ranging vocabulary and sentences.

Convey convincing and original voices in your writing

Learning objectives
You will learn how to
- use particular techniques to convey different tones and styles of voice
- make your voice stand out through original approaches.

Assessment objectives
- English Language AO5, AO6

How can you develop an original and engaging tone of voice?

Getting you thinking

What does it mean to be able to write in an original or distinctive 'voice'? In essence, it means that your language has a particular flavour or tone which is unlike anyone else's. It means that, as you write, your reader feels that they can almost hear you speaking, expressing yourself in your own individual style.

Here is an extract from a humorous column that appeared in *The Guardian*. In this extract, the author complains to his wife that he can't get into his study at home because the house is being decorated.

> 'Why don't you take the dogs out?' she says.
> 'I hate the dogs,' I say. Really, I only hate one of the dogs, but they come as a package.
> 'Go on,' she says. 'It will be good for you.'
> I decide she is right. The park is sunny and quiet, and no one is painting it.
>
> Tim Dowling, 'Hounded out', from *The Guardian*, 22 March 2014

1. Based on the evidence here, what does Tim Dowling (the 'I' of the article) think about his dogs?

2. What does the extract suggest about his relationship with his wife?

3. How would you describe his tone of voice in this extract? Think about the title and what you can infer from it.

Explore the skills

Even though this is a very short extract, we begin to get quite a good sense of the author's voice, and from that, his feelings.

What he writes	What it suggests about the writer	What distinctive features of 'voice' it has
'…I only hate one of the dogs, but they come as a package.'	He has a soft side, and a sense of humour: even though he dislikes one of the dogs it wouldn't be fair to punish the others.	This comment is an 'aside' – as if explaining for the reader's benefit something he wouldn't tell his wife.
'Go on. It'll be good for you.' (his wife)	He would like to be seen as in charge (saying he hates the dogs) but actually does what she says.	The short, clipped conversation with his wife is like a little playscript within the article.
'The park is sunny and quiet and no one is painting it.'	He hasn't quite forgotten how grumpy he is about the decorators.	Slightly absurd idea of someone 'painting' the park adds to the dry, grumpy sense of humour.

Readers of Tim Dowling's regular columns know that they are going to get **vignettes** of his life, which are probably embellished or invented to entertain the reader or make comments about everyday life.

Key term

vignettes: short scenes that give a strong impression of a character or event

 4 Write a similar paragraph in which you recount a conversation with a member of your family or a friend on a particular topic or event you feel grumpy about.

Include:

- a snippet of the conversation
- an aside or comment which is intended for the reader.

Develop the skills

Writers can use other techniques to let us into their world, and create a distinctive tone and style. Read this extract from a review by Xan Brooks of *The Amazing Spider-Man 2* that appeared in *The Guardian*.

> Childhood heroes never die, they simply outgrow us, outlive us, and transfer their attentions to the generations that follow. Even Spider-Man, whom I loved as a kid, has now long since moved on. He's taken the Hollywood shilling, embraced three-dimensions and pitched himself squarely at the multiplex crowd. By rights it should be all over between us.
> Yet *The Amazing Spider-Man 2* turns out to be so savvy, punchy and dashing that it won't be denied. It's the thread that won't break and the yarn which still binds.
>
> Xan Brooks, '*The Amazing Spider-Man 2* review', from *The Guardian*, 9 April 2014

Here, the distinctiveness of Xan Brooks's voice comes from a central, **extended metaphor** to convey his point of view about Spiderman, both as a film now, and in the past.

5 What is that metaphor used here? Think about some of the key phrases used:

- 'transfer their attentions'
- 'it should be all over between us...'
- 'it won't be denied...'

6 Can you find any other phrases or references in the text that fit the same metaphor?

7 What does the metaphor tell us about Xan Brooks' feelings about the film *Spiderman*?

8 Xan Brooks uses a particularly powerful metaphor in his final sentence to explain his connection with Spiderman. It builds on the original idea but also **alludes** to new ones.

  a What other metaphor or image does he use?
  b Why is it such a well-chosen one?
  c How is the final part of it a pun?

9 Think about a soft toy, gadget or game you were obsessed with when you were 6 or 7 years' old. Write a paragraph in which you refer to the item as if it was a disease or addiction.

Start:

> I couldn't get enough of it...it consumed me...

In this final extract from an article in *The Guardian* by Tim Lott, the distinctive voice of the writer is turned towards something more serious: friendship.

> **Key term**
>
> **extended metaphor:** a comparison between two ideas which is developed over the course of a text, rather than in one single example

> **Key term**
>
> **alludes:** makes a passing reference to other stories or ideas, often in an indirect or subtle way

> The nature of friendship changes, and you have to change with it. Once, hopefully, I fascinated my friends and charmed them. After 40 years, I am sure I often bore them – and that is inevitable. A good friendship, like a good marriage, ceases after a while to be a mutual entertainment society and becomes instead a sorority or fraternity of battle-scarred veterans. We are still here, we still enjoy being around each other, and we treasure our shared histories. This is something precious, even if it isn't always a laugh riot.
>
> Is there a secret to long friendships? Simply this – an absence of pride. Too many falter on stubbornness or the determination to hold on to offence. Successful ones rely on humility and the recognition of human fallibility. These are not merely useful attributes. They are the heart and soul of friendship.
>
> Tim Lott, 'Good friends are hard to find – and even harder to keep', from *The Guardian*, 13 August 2014

Tim Lott draws on some of the techniques used earlier, for example metaphor, in the comparison of friendship to marriage, and even war ('battle-scarred veterans'). But his distinctive voice comes as much from *how* he expresses these ideas.

10 Lott makes simple assertions or statements of belief, which sound rather like advice given by a counsellor. For example, 'The nature of friendship changes, and you have to change with it'.

   a Can you find two other examples of similar statements of advice or explanation?

   b What do these statements tell us about Tim Lott as a person?

Apply the skills

11 Before starting the task below, think about how you can build a distinctive and original voice by looking back over the three extracts you have read.

'Friendships come and go throughout life and we exaggerate their value. If we lose touch with or forget about childhood friends, we will gain new ones in adult lives. It is no big deal.'

Write the first three paragraphs of a feature article (with a suitable title or heading) for a magazine expressing your point of view on this subject.

Checklist for success

- Use a small vignette or moment from your life and embellish it (even if you don't mean it!), perhaps including asides to the reader.
- Build an extended metaphor around friends and the passing of time.
- Express your views in clear statements or assertions.

Check your progress:

- ▲▲ I can select from a range of distinctive voices and language techniques to create a convincing, original voice of my own.

- ▲ I can recognise different styles of voice in texts and choose from some of the techniques writers use to create my own text.

- ▲ I can write a convincing article that has a clear style and a sense of voice.

Manipulate structure to create effects in point-of-view writing

Learning objectives
You will learn how to
- consider a range of inventive ways to open point-of-view articles
- adapt or alter structures of texts for different effects.

Assessment objectives
- English Language AO5, AO6

How can you structure points in an opinion piece to create impact in an original, yet clear way?

Getting you thinking

It is important to get your viewpoint across clearly and in a logical way so that the reader fully understands it, but this can potentially lead to rather dull writing. Therefore, it is important that you experiment with alternative ways of conveying your key ideas.

Read the opening three paragraphs to an article in *The Guardian* by George Monbiot about a particular pesticide.

Here's our choice. We wait and see if a class of powerful pesticides, made by Bayer and Syngenta, is indeed pushing entire ecosystems to oblivion, or suspend their use while proper trials are conducted. The natural world versus two chemical companies: how hard can this be?

Papers published over the past few weeks suggest that these neonicotinoids, pesticides implicated in killing or disabling bees, have similar effects on much of life on Earth. On land and in water, these neurotoxins appear to be degrading entire food chains. Licensed before sufficient tests were conducted, they are now the world's most widely used pesticides. We are just beginning to understand what we've walked into.

A paper in Nature last week showed a strong correlation between neonicotinoid concentrations and the decline of birds such as swallows, skylarks, yellowhammers, wagtails, starlings and whitethroats. It couldn't demonstrate causation, but it was elegantly designed to exclude competing factors. The precipitous loss of insects caused by neonicotinoids is the simplest and most obvious explanation, as all these birds depend on insects to feed their young. Where the chemical was heavily used, bird populations fell by 3.5% a year; where it was not, they held up. At this rate, it doesn't take long to engineer a world without song.

George Monbiot, 'Ban neonicotinoids now – to avert another silent spring', from *The Guardian*, 16 July 2014

1. What is Monbiot's viewpoint about pesticides?

2. Why do you think he began with the first paragraph rather than the second or third?

3. Why does he use such a wide range of technical language related to the topic?

Explore the skills

By carefully considering what to **foreground**, and what to use as supporting evidence, you can vary the tone and impact of your point-of-view writing.

For example, Monbiot's opening paragraph contains more 'emotional triggers' (phrases or sentences designed to create an emotive response in the reader) than factual evidence.

Key term

foreground: bring to the front or start

Opening sentence: short, sharp topic sentence grabs our attention

Second sentence: explains the choice (suspend the use of chemicals or let companies do what they want)

Third sentence: emotive rhetorical question telling us there is no choice, really, but to stop the use of chemicals.

However, by using technical terms, such as 'ecosystem', he also establishes his status as an expert.

4 Which sentences in the second and third paragraphs are included for rhetorical effect – to trigger sympathy – rather than add new evidence?

5 What technical language is used to support his argument?

6 A student writing on a similar topic has drafted this paragraph.

> *Around my village, there is an unbroken stretch of brown earth which covers a vast area of land. Nature is a monochrome canvas, empty of life. The hedges that once divided the fields are gone, and so is the wildlife that lived in them. Everything has retreated in the face of intensive farming to feed our need for ever-cheaper produce.*

   a Identify the 'emotional trigger' sentence.
   b Where would it be better placed? (Does it work best as a summary sentence, or as a starting point?)
   c Rewrite the paragraph with the 'emotional trigger' in its new location.

7 Now add your own 'emotional trigger' sentence either to the front or end of this paragraph.

> Should we allow farmers to continue to farm intensively to supply our need for cheaper food, or should the government introduce some sort of target number of hedges per acre? With diverse agriculture, comes diverse natural habitats which, in turn, produces varied life-forms.

Either begin with a short, sharp statement addressing the reader (as Monbiot does)
or use a rhetorical question at the end
or use an emotive statement which makes your viewpoint clear
or use a combination of two or more of these.

Develop the skills

Making your argument compelling is not just a matter of selecting and positioning particular sentences in your paragraphs. You also need to consider the overall structure of your text.

- Monbiot begins by introducing the reader to a scenario or problem – 'Here's our choice...'.
- He continues with general evidence about the harmful impact of particular pesticides.
- His third paragraph deals with one report in detail – which focuses on birds.

In this way, he 'drills down' from the general to the specific.

8 Read the following task and consider how you might approach the structure of the article.

> 'Supermarkets should only stock seasonal or local food products. Flying or transporting food halfway around the world makes no sense economically or socially.'
>
> Write an opinion piece for a broadsheet paper in which you explain your point of view.

Unlike newspaper reports, opinion pieces do not always reveal their main viewpoint straight away. In fact, writers sometimes begin with a related event, anecdote or other short account in order to 'draw the reader in'.

Here is a range of points and ideas that could be included in the article.

- Point about the negative impact of global trade on local producers.
- A personal anecdote about a recent visit to a local supermarket.
- A description of someone on the other side of the world working on a farm.
- Point about the way having so much food choice has changed people's expectations and wants.
- Point about how eating seasonal produce links us more closely to weather, times of year and our local community.

9 Add any other negative points and alternative ideas to the list.

10 List the *positive* aspects of having access to global produce at any time.

Now consider how you might organise your ideas. Here are three potential ways of doing so:

Strong, single **polemical** viewpoint	**Balanced** discussion, but which comes down on one side by the end	Strong persuasive article which **acknowledges the other side**
No reference to alternative or other side of argument	Reference to both sides of argument – dealing with first in first half of article, and the second after that	Reference to other argument, but dismissed each time an alternative point is mentioned
Intro Paragraph 1: negative point A Paragraph 2: negative point B Paragraphs 3–6: negative point C, D, E, etc. Conclusion	Intro Paragraphs 1–3: negative points A, B, C, etc. Paragraphs 4–6: positive points: A, B, C, etc. Conclusion: final viewpoint	Intro Paragraph 1: negative and positive points A addressed Paragraph 2: negative and positive points B addressed Paragraphs 3–6: remaining points dealt with in turn Conclusion

11 Look back at your key points (good or bad) and choose one of the three structures from the table. Consider how your choice will affect the style or tone of your article. Make brief notes on these questions:

- Will it read like Monbiot's? Or have a less polemical tone?
- How might this affect how you begin your article?

Key term

polemical: sharply critical attack

Apply the skills

12 Now you can take the earlier task a stage further.

'Supermarkets should only stock seasonal or local food products. Flying or transporting food halfway around the world makes no sense economically or socially.'

Plan the opening three paragraphs to your opinion piece for a broadsheet paper in which you explain your point of view. Then write your three paragraphs.

Checklist for success

- What to include in the opening paragraph – and its style.
- How it will relate to the next two paragraphs. (Will they build/provide more detail? Or will they deal with an entirely new point or side of the argument?)
- What order of sentences will create the impact you want in each paragraph, for example, could you end with rhetorical questions?

Check your progress:

- I can select from a range of structures and use them in inventive and engaging ways in my point-of-view writing.
- I can consider some different structures and choose one that makes my point-of-view clear and coherent.
- I can write in a structured manner using clear paragraphs to build a persuasive argument.

Match style and tone to purpose and audience

Learning objective
You will learn how to
- match your style and tone to the subject and purpose in a convincing way.

Assessment objectives
- English Language AO5, AO6

How can you pitch your style perfectly to match the task?

Getting you thinking

Read this extract from *The Guardian* by Harry Leslie Smith. It is from an article about the government's plan to allow companies to hold on to personal data about people.

For the government to have private corporations store so much information about us without earnest, prolonged debate and reflection by parliament is more than an affront to our country's long-held belief in privacy, in our right to freedom of thought and movement; it is an affront to human progress. Since the dark ages, human society has fought to remove the yoke of state and feudal control. Freedom is the most sacred burden that all people must fight to preserve. The right to privacy, to worship, to assemble, to be a member of a union, to dissent, to choose, and to love and be loved regardless of one's sexual orientation, are all at risk if this bill becomes law. It took centuries of struggle for our nation to acquire the attributes of a civilised and just society. But they can vanish in a moment if our elected representatives fail to defend those rights in parliament.

The data retention and investigatory powers bill will not make British citizens safer in their everyday lives, nor will it protect us from terrorists, organised crime or keep our children out of harm's way. All it will do is put a leash on the human spirit and deaden the hearts of those who desire to live in a free and liberal nation. It is incumbent upon our parliament to debate this bill and mitigate its omnipotence. Otherwise this new set of surveillance laws will be used to draw an **iron curtain** across freedom and democracy in Britain.

Harry Leslie Smith, 'This surveillance bill puts our hard-won freedom in peril', from *The Guardian*, 11 July 2014

Glossary

iron curtain: a phrase used to describe the division between so-called 'free' countries in the West, and Communist countries in the East after World War 2

1. Write brief answers to these questions.

   a What is the issue Harry Leslie Smith wishes to address here?

   b What is his purpose?

   c How would you describe the tone of the article?

   d Who is his likely audience here?

Explore the skills

In tackling a serious issue, Smith uses an appropriately serious tone. He uses powerful, hard-hitting but formal language to express the vital importance of freedom both in the past and present, for example:

- 'an **affront** to human progress'
- 'the **attributes** of a free and just society'.

He could have written: 'two fingers up to progress' or 'the best bits of living free and easy…' but this would have undermined the sense that he is an informed, thoughtful writer.

2. Can you find where Smith has used more powerful, formal usages for these words or phrases?

> 'For years, people have tried hard to get rid of leaders and the rich controlling them…'
>
> 'MPs have got a big, big duty to talk about this bill…'

The persuasive power of the article is also seen in the rhetorical flourishes of his language, as shown here.

Repeated verb patterns, creating an almost poetic effect:	Clear statements of belief, for example, in the repeated use of the verb 'will':
'The right *to privacy, to worship, to assemble, to be a member of a union, to dissent, to choose,* and *to love and be loved* regardless of one's sexual orientation, are all at risk if this bill becomes law.'	'The data retention and investigatory powers bill *will not* make British citizens safer in their everyday lives, *nor will it* protect us from terrorists, organised crime or keep our children out of harm's way.'

3. Can you identify two other occasions where Smith uses repeated patterns of vocabulary or verbs for rhetorical effect?

4. Now try something similar yourself.

   Imagine you wish to argue the opposite: that it is necessary for organisations to keep personal information as it will provide help in catching terrorists and criminals.

   Here is your first draft, but it does not sound sufficiently powerful or have the rhetorical effect of Smith's article.

> It's really important that you can find out about what villains are up to or get info on terrorists who have ideas up their sleeve for attacking the UK. The country's safety is the issue, I reckon, and it would be a bit silly to ignore this. In fact, my and your safety is also an issue. This bill could make life a bit safer for all of us. Better for you and safer for your family. Also, people at work or those who run the country.

a Start by listing any words or phrases that don't seem sufficiently powerful or assertive. (Can you get rid of or replace weak adverbs, adjectives or nouns? Could you use 'will' or 'must' anywhere?)

b Select any sentences that could be combined into a more fluent, flowing single sentence, with repeated verb patterns as in Smith's article.

c Now rewrite the text.

Develop the skills

Part of Smith's rhetorical power also comes from using appropriate metaphors. He talks about:

- 'the **yoke** of state and feudal control': 'yoke' means the harness used to control horses when ploughing in the past

- '...this new set of surveillance laws will be used to draw an iron curtain across freedom and democracy in Britain.' As mentioned earlier, 'iron curtain' was a famous image used to describe the barriers put up between countries after World War 2.

5 Why do you think he uses these somewhat old-fashioned or historical terms? What does it add to the tone of the article?

6 Can you find where he uses a further metaphor (similar to 'yoke') to describe how the proposed bill will hold back freedom?

7 Here is a further extract from the contrasting article. Copy and complete the paragraph, adding suitably powerful metaphors to make your point.

> We need this Bill so we can shine a light into the
> ....of terrorism.
> Without it, criminals will be able to unlock the
> ....of government. Britain needs
> to remain a..out of the
> reach of those who wish to do us harm or destroy our liberties.

Images are being recorded for the safety of pupils, staff and visitors and for the prevention and detection of crime.

Apply the skills

8 Read the statements below and complete the task that follows it.

'All schools for all ages should routinely be fitted with surveillance cameras. Only through this action can we ensure the safety and security of staff, students and visitors.'

Write the first three paragraphs of an article for a broadsheet paper in which you explain your views on this issue, following the three steps below:

- first, consider the topic; what tone and style should you adopt for it? Is the subject a light-hearted one, or something that requires 'serious' treatment?
- plan your paragraphs, jotting down the key points you wish to make
- draft your opening paragraphs.

Checklist for success

- Consider how you can create rhetorical impact through the patterns of words, phrases and sentences you use.
- Think about how you can create impact through the strength or power of the vocabulary you select.
- Consider how the use of metaphor might add weight or conviction to your argument.

Check your progress:

▲▲ I can create a compelling and convincing argument through careful selection of language and linguistic patterns to match my tone, audience and purpose.

▲▲ I can use a range of suitable rhetorical effects and patterns to make my argument clear and convincing.

▲ I can write in a tone that matches audience and purpose to create a clear point-of-view article.

Apply your skills to an English Language task

Learning objectives

You will learn to

- apply the key skills from this chapter to an English Language task
- reflect on your progress through looking at different responses to the task.

Assessment objectives

- English Language AO5, AO6

Responding to an English Language task

1 Read this task and consider how you would respond to it.

'Solitude is damaging: everyone needs others for companionship and communication.'

Write an article for a student section in a broadsheet newspaper in which you explain your point of view on this statement.

Reflecting on your progress

2 Read the following response to this task. As you read, think about what the student has done well and what advice they might need in order to make more progress.

Response 1

I have been considering becoming a hermit. Yeah – the idea of a simple cave on a barren hillside, growing my hair long is sometimes very appealing. Ok, I'm not sure my mum would approve (she gets worried if I catch the bus on my own) but the general idea makes sense.

The truth is I am far too popular. Well, when I say 'popular' perhaps what I really mean is that I have to deal with lots of people telling me what to do. For example, take my English teacher; here's a typical conversation:

'Ah, Simon…' (that's my teacher speaking, not me – we're not that close)

'Yes, sir'

'Um, have you done that homework yet? The one I've reminded you about a trillion times?'

'Sorry, sir…I…um…well the truth is that I'm not going to need it when I take up residence in Numero 1, Cave 3, Side of the Hill…'

Then there's that gang of girls in Year 8…always chasing me.

surprising opening paragraph does not address issue immediately

humour used to create sense of voice/exaggerated persona of writer

dialogue, probably invented, used to build the 'angle' being pursued

Admittedly, they want to beat me up, but you see what I mean? If I could only get away.

Solitude has lots of pluses. I yearn for the moment when I can shut my bedroom door, chase the cat off the bed, close the curtains and listen to something depressing on my phone. I yearn to forget the fact that my brother will soon be home from work and will invade my space… well, legally speaking his as well as he has a bed in here too … and force me to talk about something trivial like how he's got the sack, or how his girlfriend has left him. No, it's perfect for a while. Just me, a monotonous keyboard and drums, and blackness. What could be better?

long paragraph develops the idea by painting a picture of the writer's own room

I also need solitude to be creative. I need the time to let my mind whirr round, all its millions of little cogs racing and rattling, fuelled by the fact that nothing else is being put into it. I need space to think about my future, the universe, the million questions that worry me on a daily basis.

metaphor takes argument in a new direction

The truth is solitude is a luxury nowadays. Humankind is never out of reach. If you turn your phone off, or don't answer the door, or refuse to 'work in a group', you're a weirdo. If you prefer to stare at the wall, walk along a path on your own, go to the cinema without half of the school, you're a loner. And, worst of all, if you don't speak loudly, or confidently, shout out your opinion or trample over everyone else's, you're a failure. You don't fit into society's view of someone who is 'useful'.

repeated rhetorical patterns

Those hermits had the right idea. A cave in a remote spot is probably the only place you can be truly, utterly yourself.

short final paragraph links back to beginning of article

Comments on Response 1

The tone slips a little uneasily between the comic and the serious in places, although the personal anecdotes communicate successfully with the readers, and the varied structure – moving from dialogue to reflection and on to further anecdotes – keeps the reader engaged. Links between ideas and within and between paragraphs are generally coherent and allow the reader to move fluently from one focus to the next. However, the mix of formal and informal does not always work.

3 How could this sample response be improved? Using the middle rung of the Check your progress ladder at the end of this chapter, think about what advice you might give to this student in order to improve their work.

4 Now read Response 2. As you read, think about what the student has done that is an improvement on Response 1, and what advice this student might need in order to make even more progress.

Response 2

Being alone damages the individual and society. As human beings, we have not been built to withstand loneliness; at the moment of our birth we are connected to someone, somewhere, and if we have company taken away from us, then we suffer. After all, why do babies react as they do when their parents leave the room?

I recall a time when I did not have many friends. I had just moved to a new school and I couldn't really settle in. I am an only child and when I came home I had to let myself in to the house, and face the emptiness. Yes, I was able to go on my laptop and contact all my old friends back in Leeds, but it wasn't the same. At those moments, the proximity of physical, human contact is vital. That's when I thought what it must be like for older citizens who live alone. Loneliness is the silent killer, the creeping fog that infects too many in society. I had had a taste of it, and it wasn't pleasant.

Of course, soon I made friends and I forgot those feelings of isolation. But I was really miserable back then. I wanted to talk to people face to face about school and the problems I was having, but there just wasn't anyone. When my parents came in, they listened while I tried to explain. But they didn't really get it. Solitude takes many forms too. You can be surrounded by others, and still feel alone. Remembering those days, I recall how I would stand in that horrible wet playground with everyone playing football around me and think: am I invisible? Has that fog of loneliness made me untouchable? Eventually this boy who's now my closest friend – Liam – came up to me. He said they needed another player in his team and asked me to join in. I didn't need to be asked twice. The fog lifted, and I turned a corner.

- clear opening statement of opinion
- direct question to readers engages their attention
- memory/anecdote supports point of view
- suggests switch to a new, but related topic
- discourse marker 'those' links back to previous paragraph
- simple, informal short sentence sums up feelings
- visual detail adds colour to the argument

I sometimes think of those people who sail around the world on their own. I mean, how do they do it? Imagine being all on your own on a vast expanse of water, literally thousands of miles from home. Just you, the boat and emptiness. Even with satellite phones and all the paraphernalia of modern communication, you basically have to accept that you're not going to see a human face for months. I couldn't do it.

new paragraph takes the argument in slightly new direction

The truth is I need company like a plant needs water. Without human contact, I wither and shrivel, become a shadow of my real self. I know not everyone feels this way — some people like their own company — but I'm definitely not one of them. Life is built on our ability to make connections, to interact with others, to exchange and argue over ideas. Without companions, who would there be to share pleasures or troubles with? Who would offer us guidance or consolation?

further extended metaphor adds emotional impact

Solitude can be a temporary relief from life's strains, but it is not a permanent solution to society's problems. On the contrary, it may well be the cause of them.

short final paragraph effectively sums up the point of view

Comments on Response 2

This is a fluent, coherent and convincing response which leaves little doubt as to the writer's point of view. The structure has been thoughtfully composed for maximum impact and presents ideas logically and persuasively. The writer also uses a range of language techniques, drawing on powerful imagery, personal experience and reflective thinking to get ideas across.

Check your progress

- I can select from a range of distinctive voices and language techniques to create a convincing, original voice of my own.

- I can select from a range of structures and use them in inventive and engaging ways in my point-of-view writing.

- I can create a compelling and convincing argument through careful selection of language and linguistic patterns to match my tone, audience and purpose.

- I can recognise different styles of voice in texts and choose from some of the techniques writers use to create my own text.

- I can consider some different structures and choose one that makes my point of view clear and coherent.

- I can use a range of suitable rhetorical effects and patterns to make my argument clear and convincing.

- I can write a convincing article that has a clear style and a sense of voice.

- I can write in a structured manner using clear paragraphs to build a persuasive argument.

- I can write in a tone that matches audience and purpose to create a clear point-of-view article.

Glossary of key terms

address: the mode of speaking to the reader (for example, direct, distant, objective)

adjectival phrase: a group of words that describe a noun

adverb: a word that changes or simplifies the meaning of a verb, and usually answers how or when an action was done (for example, angrily, later)

alliteration: repetition of a sound, usually (but not always) at the start of a sequence of words

alludes: makes a passing reference to other stories or ideas, often in an indirect or subtle way

allusions: references to other stories or texts

analogies: extended comparisons made between two ideas or experiences

anecdotes: short personal stories designed to add humour or illustrate a point

bildungsroman: a genre of narrative fiction where a character develops into emotional maturity via overcoming a series of obstacles and learning some hard lessons about life, themselves, and the right moral path in order to attain wisdom and happiness by the end of the novel

caesura: is a break or pause in the flow of a line, often used to emphasise key ideas, words, or moments

cinquain: a five line poem invented by Adelaide Crapsey which has a structure of 2, 4, 6, 8, 2 syllable lines

clause: a group of words that contains a verb; a clause may form part of a sentence or it may be a complete sentence in itself

complex sentence: develops ideas in a simple sentence and adds detail and information in subsections known as subordinate clauses

compound-complex sentence: a complex sentence connected to a simple sentence by a conjunction

compound sentence: two simple sentences with linked ideas joined together with conjunctions (and, or, but)

connotations: ideas, images or associations brought to mind by a word or phrase

conventions: recognisable or accepted features of a particular genre

diapason: a full, beautiful, musical sound

enjambment: continuing a sentence or clause over a line break to delay closure and increase anticipation

evaluate: to judge the significance of something based on analysis of evidence

extended metaphor: a metaphor developed over a sequence of text

faxes: an early form of technical communication in the 1980s

figurative language: words or phrases that represent or symbolise other ideas, not just literal ones

first person: mode of narrating which uses 'I' to tell the story

foreground: bring to the front or start

genre: category or type of text, such as 'detective' or 'chick lit'

guineas: old coins, worth just over one pound

imagery: language that creates vivid pictures

inferential reading: reading beyond the surface or literal meaning by considering what is implied or suggested by a text

interpretation: a particular way of looking at or understanding something

iron curtain: a phrase used to describe the division between so-called 'free' countries in the West, and communist countries in the East after World War 2

ironic: pointing out the difference between the surface and the reality of a situation

libations: pouring out of drink as an offering to a god or in memory of the dead

literal: the surface or obvious meaning

minor sentence: a sentence that lacks one or more of the elements that go to make up a full sentence, for example, a subject or a main verb

modification: when the mental picture we have of the noun is altered by the choice of the adjective which accompanies it

narrative perspective: the point of view or position of the person telling a story to the reader

op-ed article: an article or essay in a newspaper, expressing the opinions or viewpoint of a writer who does not work for that newspaper

personification: a type of metaphor where an inanimate object is given human characteristics such as emotions

phrase: two or more words forming a complete expression or forming part of a sentence

plurality: more than one, but not infinite

polemical: sharply critical attack

prepositions: words which are used to show the relation of one noun or pronoun to another in a sentence

quinine: a treatment for malaria

semantic field: a group or collection of words that have a similar meaning or create similar ideas in the mind of the reader

simile: form of comparison using 'as' or 'like'

simple sentence: presents one idea. It will have one verb or verb phrase and contain one action, event or state

symbolise: represent

syndetic list: uses a conjunction, most commonly 'and', within its list of items; an asyndetic list does not

synonyms: words or phrases with identical or very close meanings

synthesise: draw together information from one or more sources

tone: suggests an attitude in the 'voice' that is 'speaking' to you in the text, for example, through the words used, the way sentences are phrased and the level of formality

volta: change of direction in a sonnet, used to mark a turn in thought

Acknowledgements

The publishers gratefully acknowledge the permissions granted to reproduce copyright material in this book. Every effort has been made to contact the holders of copyright material, but if any have been inadvertently overlooked, the Publisher will be pleased to make the necessary arrangements at the first opportunity.

pp60–61 The Road to Wigan Pier by George Orwell (Copyright © George Orwell, 1937) reprinted by permission of Bill Hamilton as the Literary Executor of the Estate of the Late Sonia Brownell Orwell. Excerpt from THE ROAD TO WIGAN PIER by George Orwell. Copyright © 1958 and renewed by the Estate of Sonia B. Orwell. Reprinted by permission of Houghton Mifflin Harcourt Publishing Company. All rights reserved.; p70 Material by Ros Barber taken from: How to Leave the World that Worships Should, by Ros Barber and published by Anvil Press Poetry, 2008. Used with permission.; p79 SWAN from the volume SWAN – Poems and Prose Poems by Mary Oliver, published by Beacon Press, Boston USA and Bloodaxe Books Ltd., UK Copyright © 20010 by Mary Oliver, used herewith by permission of the Charlotte Sheedy Literary Agency, Inc.; pp16–17 Extract from: If nobody speaks of remarkable things © Jon McGregor. Published by Bloomsbury in 2003 and used with kind permission from Bloomsbury Plc and The Wylie Agency (UK) Ltd. Excerpt from IF NOBODY SPEAKS OF REMARKABLE THINGS by Jon McGregor. Copyright © 2003. Reprinted by permission of Houghton Mifflin Harcourt Publishing Company. All rights reserved.; p29 Excerpt from Rebecca by Daphne du Maurier reproduced with permission of Curtis Brown, © The Chichester Partnership, 1938; pp85–88 Excerpts from Pack of Cards, copyright © 1978, 1986 by Penelope Lively. Used by permission of Grove/Atlantic, Inc. and Penguin, with kind permission from David Higham Associates. Any third party use of this material, outside of this publication, is prohibited.; pp126–127 Excerpt from Dress Your Family in Corduroy and Denim by David Sedaris, Abacus 2004. Used with permission from Don Congdon Associates, Inc.; p24 Virginia by T. S. Eliot taken from The Complete Poems and plays T.S. Eliot (2004) reprinted by permission of the publishers Faber and Faber; pp90–92 At a potato digging taken from New Selected Poems 1966-1987 (1990) reprinted by permission of the publishers Faber and Faber; pp153–155 The Rain Horse by Ted Hughes taken from Modern Short Stories, Book 1, edited by Jim Hunter (1974) reprinted by permission of the publishers Faber and Faber; pp72–74 The Sound of the Shell taken from Lord of the Flies by William Golding (1997) reprinted by permission of the publishers Faber and Faber; p136 Incendiary by Vernon Scannell taken from Collected Poems 1950-1993 (2013) reprinted by permission of the publishers Faber and Faber; p143 Background Material, by Tony Harrison (1984) reprinted by permission of the publishers Faber and Faber; p12 Harry Potter and the Philosopher's Stone: Copyright © J.K. Rowling 1997; p135 Children in Wartime used with kind permission from Isobel Thrilling; p13 Excerpts from THE WAVES by Virginia Woolf. Copyright 1931 by Houghton Mifflin Harcourt Publishing Company. Copyright © renewed 1959 by Leonard Woolf. Reprinted by permission of Houghton Mifflin Harcourt Publishing Company and The Society of Authors as the Literary Representative of the Estate of Virginia Woolf. All rights reserved.; pp116–117 From THE KITE RUNNER by Khaled Hosseini, copyright © 2003 by Khaled Hosseini. Used by permission of Riverhead Books, an imprint of Penguin Group (USA) LLC, Penguin Random House Canada and Bloomsbury Publishing Plc.; p131 Below the Green Corrie taken from The Poems of Norman MacCaig, edited by Ewen MacCaig. Published by Polygon (an imprint of Birlinn Ltd), 2009. Used with permission from Birlinn Ltd.; p113 From STRANDS by Jean Sprackland, Published by Jonathan Cape, Reprinted by permission of The Random House Group Limited; pp150–151 From HIGH FIDELITY by Nick Hornby. Published by Indigo, 1996. Reprinted by permission of Penguin Books Ltd.; pp64–67 From HOW TO BE A WOMAN by Caitlin Moran. Published by Ebury Press, Reprinted by permission of The Random House Group Limited.; pp48–49, 104 Copyright Guardian News & Media Ltd 2011; p138 Copyright Guardian News & Media Ltd 2000; p166, 167, 168–169, 179, 174 Copyright Guardian News & Media Ltd 2014; p44 Excerpt from 'My London, and Welcome to it' by AA Gill. © The New York Times, 27 April, 2012.; p104 © Telegraph Media Group Limited 2011

The publishers would like to thank the following for permission to use reproduce pictures in these pages:

Cover images © Skylines/Shutterstock.com, Stocksnapper/Shutterstock.com

p8, left: bierchen/Shutterstock.com, right: Pakhnyushchy/Shutterstock.com; p10: © nobleIMAGES/ Alamy; p13: Stephen Coburn/Shutterstock.com; p14: © AF archive/Alamy; p16-17: MIMOHE/ Shutterstock.com; p18: Hulton Archive/Getty Images; p22, left: © Kirk Norbury/Alamy, right: The Bridgeman Art Library/Getty Images; p24: © Susan Isakson/Alamy; p27: © Agencja Fotograficzna Caro/Alamy; p29: © Realimage/Alamy; p30: Guillermo del Olmo/Shutterstock.com; p32: © Mary Evans Picture Library/Alamy; p37: DEA Picture Library/Getty Images; p39, top: Pani Ayanna/Shutterstock. com, centre: Balefire/Shutterstock.com, bottom left: Jaromir Urbanek/Shutterstock.com, bottom right: irin-k/Shutterstock.com; p40: Private Collection/Photo © Agnew's, London/Bridgeman Images; p43: Louvre, Paris, France/Bridgeman Images; p44-45: Alex Fradkin/Getty Images; p46: Leeds Museums and Galleries (Leeds Art Gallery)/Bridgeman Images; p49: Andre Coelho/Globo/Getty Images; p50: British Library/Robana/Rex Features; p51: Private Collection/Bridgeman Images; p60-61: George W. Hales/ Fox Photos/Getty Images; p62: © SuperStock/Alamy; p64: © epa european pressphoto agency b.v./ Alamy; p66: mikeledray/Shutterstock.com; p69: Stephen Rees/Shutterstock.com; p70: Hamiza Bakirci/ Shutterstock.com; p73: © AF archive/Alamy; p74: holbox/Shutterstock.com; p79: Nneirda/Shutterstock. com; p81: Gabriella Wetli/Shutterstock.com; p84, left: Private Collection/Photo © Christie's Images/ Bridgeman Images, right: Mary Evans Picture Library; p86-87: © Andreas von Einsiedel/Alamy; p88: AlexussK/Shutterstock.com; p91: © Walters Art Museum, Baltimore, USA/Bridgeman Images; p92-93: © Picture Partners/Alamy; p95: © Moviestore Collection Ltd/Alamy; p96: Everett Collection/Rex Features; p97: © Pictorial Press Ltd/Alamy; p98: Kean Collection/Getty Images; p104: © Photos 12/ Alamy; p105: detail from Mary Wollstonecraft (Mrs William Godwin), c.1790-1, by John Opie, © Tate, London 2014; p106: © The Estate of the Artist, reproduced with kind permission (photo: Private Collection/Bridgeman Images); p108: Private Collection/Bridgeman Images; p112: © Image Source Salsa/Alamy; p115: Albanpix Ltd/Rex Features; p117: © AF archive/Alamy; p120-121: © Bettmann/ Corbis; p126: © AF archive/Alamy; p127: Jewel Samad/AFP/Getty Images; p128: BrAt82/Shutterstock. com; p129: © Mary Evans Picture Library/Alamy; p130-131: © Andrew Fox/Alamy; p132-133: © Roland Gerth/Corbis; p134 left: Carolyn Franks/Shutterstock.com; p134 right: Nattika/Shutterstock.com; p135: © World History Archive/Alamy; p136: Jasiek03/Shutterstock.com; p138: Richard Heathcote/ Getty Images; p139: Private Collection/© The British Sporting Art Trust/Bridgeman Images; p142: ND/ Roger Viollet/Getty Images; p143: © Luisa Fumi/Alamy; p148: Hans Engbers/Shutterstock.com; p151: © PHOVOIR/Alamy; p152: © Malcolm Schuyl/Alamy; p154: Knumina Studios/Shutterstock.com; p157: Roger-Viollet/TopFoto; p158: kenny1/Shutterstock.com; p160: © Aquascopic/Alamy; p165: Matthew Dixon/Shutterstock.com; p166: Eric Isselee/Shutterstock.com; p168: © AF archive/Alamy; p170: Klagyivik Viktor/Shutterstock.com; p174: Thomas Trutschel/Photothek/Getty Images; p177: © Radharc Images/Alamy; p178: © Phanie/Alamy; p181: © Network Photographers/Alamy

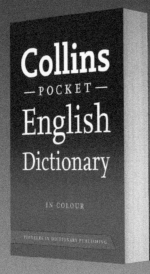

Notes

Notes

Notes